Advance Praise for Bronner

"The words of this book have truly left me speechless. Only the power and grace of God could sustain and bring comfort in the deepest of hurt. As a father myself, I can't fathom the pain of losing one of my children. I believe this book Sherri has written will bring great healing to so many who have experienced great loss. It's an honor to call Rick and Sherri Burgess my friends."
—CHRIS TOMLIN, Grammy Award-winning Christian recording artist

"As a quadriplegic, I have often said, 'God permits what he hates to accomplish that which he loves.' My friends Rick and Sherri understand that hard truth so painfully well. In this remarkable book, they show us that true wisdom is trusting God even when all seems dark. It's why *Bronner* is such a wise and good guide in your journey to grasp God's goodness in your pain. Read it and you will be blessed!"
—JONI EARECKSON TADA, Joni and Friends International Disability Center, award-winning author of over 50 books

"No one escapes life unscathed. Everyone faces tragedy. Rick and Sherri did. They did so with faith. We are wise to learn from their example. Their story inspires us to face our challenges by facing God first."
—MAX LUCADO, *New York Times* best-selling author

"*Bronner* tells the heart-wrenching but ultimately encouraging story of God's steadfast love for the Burgess family during its darkest hour. This book testifies to how the Lord gave them 'a crown of beauty instead of ashes, the oil of joy instead of mourning, and a garment of praise instead of a spirit of despair. (Isaiah 61:3)'"
—JIM DALY, president, Focus on the Family

"'Thank You, Lord, for trusting me with something so great that I would be asked to give up what You gave up—a son.' These are the powerful words of Sherri Burgess in *Bronner*. To a Christian culture saturated with the notion that material and physical well being are at the center of God's will for our lives, such words are jarring. It just so happens that they also find resonance in Scripture."
—LARRY ALEX TAUNTON, author of *The Grace Effect*

"*Bronner* is a moving work that vividly portrays how the Burgess family trusted God to carry them through tremendous tragedy. The raw emotion recounting the life-changing event and the real transparency of the struggle to move forward afterwards grip both mind and heart as the reader travels through their experience. The Burgess journey is a powerful plea for all to know real peace and real life-sustaining hope that can only be found in Jesus. So well written, *Bronner* is a great read that will have lasting impact on the lives of all who learn his story."

—TARRA DAWSON, wife of Scott Dawson,
Scott Dawson Evangelistic Association

"'God had something different in mind.' If you understand these words by Sherri Burgess you must read *Bronner*. This is an honest story of the very real sting of loss yet against the profound backdrop of a very real hope. Rick and Sherri Burgess know and offer a beautiful Jesus who is empowering, comforting, and sufficient."

—DR. ED LITTON, senior pastor of Redemption Church in
Saraland, Alabama, and KATHY LITTON, national consultant for the
North American Mission Board

"*Bronner* is a deep look into the heart of a mother who chases hard after the heart of her Heavenly Father, who has clung to Him in the darkest of nights and found Him so very faithful. Sherri's words have touched me in the deepest parts of my heart and spirit, and there's not a doubt in my mind that the Lord will convict, inspire, and challenge through Sherri's obedience to tell His story. Beautifully written, Christ-centered, and saturated with truth, *Bronner* is truly an offering to the Lord and to the Body of Christ. You'll be changed after you read it. I know I have been."

—SOPHIE HUDSON, author of *Home is Where My People Are* and *A Little Salty to Cut the Sweet*

"Not only will this book be a blessing for those who have lost a child, but it will give hope when the inevitable 'Why does God allow bad things to happen to good people?' question comes up. It is a compelling and inspirational story about how Rick and Sherri Burgess used such an unthinkable tragedy to reach and help so many others."

—DON KEITH, best-selling author of 28 books, including *The Ship That Wouldn't Die* and *Mattie C.'s Boy*

BRONNER

A JOURNEY TO UNDERSTAND

Sherri Burgess

NEW HOPE® PUBLISHERS

Gospel-Centered. Missions-Driven.

BIRMINGHAM, ALABAMA

New Hope® Publishers
PO Box 12065
Birmingham, AL 35202-2065

NewHopePublishers.com
New Hope Publishers is a division of WMU®.

Library of Congress Cataloging-in-Publication Data

Names: Burgess, Sherri, 1970- author.
Title: Bronner : a journey to understand / Sherri Burgess.
Description: Birmingham, Alabama : New Hope Publishers, 2016.
Identifiers: LCCN 2015037033 | ISBN 9781625915009 (sc)
Subjects: LCSH: Children--Death--Religious aspects--Christianity. |
    Consolation. | Mother and child.
Classification: LCC BV4907 .B825 2016 | DDC 248.8/66092--dc23 LC record
available at http://lccn.loc.gov/2015037033

Cover Designer: Marc Whitaker, MTW Design
Interior Page Designer: Glynese Northam

ISBN-10: 1-62591-500-4
ISBN-13: 978-1-62591-500-9

N164109 • 0216 • 5M3

To the Lord Jesus Christ, who both commanded and enabled me by the power of the Holy Spirit to write this book—may this be an acceptable sacrifice of love and gratitude to the Father for His great mercy on this, your humble servant.

And to my family, whose sacrifice of time with Bronner now will result in praise and glory and honor at the revelation of Jesus Christ.

I waited patiently for the LORD;

he inclined to me and heard my cry.

He drew me up from the pit of destruction,

out of the miry bog,

and set my feet upon a rock,

making my steps secure.

He put a new song in my mouth,

a song of praise to our God.

Many will see and fear,

and put their trust in the LORD.

—PSALM 40:1–3

CONTENTS

PREFACE

In setting out to write this book, I wanted to introduce you to my sweet Bronner. He was only two and a half when he went to heaven. I never say "died" because I don't feel that he has. I truly see him as going on to another place. Bronner didn't cease to exist. He has been transported to another land, distant and mysterious in that I have never been there before, nor can I go there right now, and haven't even the vaguest idea when I might be able to go, but also the most assured and concrete of places in that I am certain of the way and long for it like no place on earth.

Heaven has my heart, my citizenship, my baby, and my God. It is the land of the living and the kingdom of light. In contrast, earth is the land of the lost and of the dying. Bronner has been found and taken to the truest place, the best place, a place many will never find even though the Lord God specifically said, "Seek, and you will find" (Matthew 7:7). Many people seek God in a way that is only palatable to their own desires. They want God to be who they want Him to be, not who He really is, and so they never find the real, true God. Many people find God's ways offensive, harsh, even arrogant. But when you seek God for who He truly is, you'll find that He is magnificent.

In times of tragedy, grief, or despair, some people grow so angry with God that they turn away from Him completely. But even in turning away, we show that we *do* have a measure of faith, for faith is this: "the assurance of things hoped for, the conviction of things not seen" (Hebrews 11:1). We believe in God, but what we are doing in turning away from Him is saying, "I don't like you. I don't like your methods, and I don't want anything to do with a God who

He had walked me through many lesser trials before. This time He was going to have to carry me, and I trusted Him to do that.

would . . . <u>fill in the blank</u>." What we are doing is *rejecting God.*

When my life's great test came to me, I already knew God in an intimate way. I called Him my Father, my Savior, my Teacher, and my Friend. He had walked me through many lesser trials before. This time He was going to have to have to carry me, and I trusted Him to do that. Why? Because I knew Him to be good. God's goodness and mercy had already been poured out by the bucketful upon this wretched creature called me. By the time I stood in that baptistery at Lakeview Baptist Church in Oxford, Alabama, at the age of 25, I already had a quarter-century's worth of sins to wash away. But as I stood there wearing a robe of white, I felt God's Spirit moving upon me with healing in His wings. And as Brother Jerry lowered me down underneath the water, my former life was vanquished. Buried with Christ. Hidden. Covered. Washed and cleansed of the former life. Rising to new life in Him.

"Therefore, if anyone is in Christ, he is a new creation. The old has passed away; behold, the new has come" (2 Corinthians 5:17).

I was a new bride at that time, figuratively (as a newly baptized believer I became part of the church, the Bride of Christ) and literally, having married my husband, Rick, just two months prior. I was also a new mom of sorts. Rick had been married before, for a short time, and had two children, Brandi and Blake. They were there at my baptism. They were five and six years old on that day, April 21, 1996. They were there again at that same small church when their little brother, Brooks, was being dedicated to the Lord. We all stood together in a circle as Brother Jerry anointed him with

Truth. That's what I wanted. That's what I got. That's what I have to tell.

oil and as we all promised to help raise him in the fear and admonition of the Lord.

It was in that little church in the small Alabama town, where Rick spent most of his childhood and where he graduated from high school, that God would anchor Himself to our family, holding us and keeping us close to His bright shores. It was there in a Bible study called *The Mind of Christ* that I had been amazed at the discovery that the Bible contains all the answers.

As a child, I remember looking up into the sky and wondering . . .

Where are You, God?
Can You see me?
Why can't I see You?
Do You love me?

I found out just how much.

And as our family continued to grow in the fear and admonition of the Lord, adding Brody, and then Bronner, my heart began to overflow with the joy of the Lord. I was soaring on the wings of an eagle. I had tasted and had seen that the Lord is good (Psalm 34:8). He is very, very good.

And then January 19, 2008 came, like a shotgun shooting me right out of the sky.

No more soaring. I wasn't even standing. I wasn't even on ground level. I was in a pit, deep and dark, but I was still holding on to someone's hand. It was the hand of the One who had lifted me up out of darkness once before, the hand of He who had Himself knit me together in my mother's womb, the gentle hand that had spoon-fed me the truth of John 3:16 but was now placing before me the meat and the bread and the wine from His Word:

Since therefore Christ suffered in the flesh, arm yourselves
with the same way of thinking, for whoever has suffered
in the flesh has ceased from sin, so as to live for the rest of

*the time in the flesh no longer for human passions but for
the will of God.*

—1 PETER 4:1–2

None of this was going to be easy. I had been torn from my baby. He was ripped away from me, and it wasn't a clean break. *After all that goodness, Lord, what are You doing? Why? We were so happy. Our family was so happy. And we were doing all that You had asked of us. My goodness! Rick was speaking at a youth retreat when it happened. Weren't we giving enough? Now, You're going to take our baby? The baby? My baby.*

I needed some answers, so I jumped in the ring and wrestled it all out with God. I wasn't going to let go of Him until He answered me, until I could make some sense of this whole matter. Until I could understand.

Now my heart responds, *Well, here I am, Lord, still standing in the ring, but instead of wrestling with You, I'm here to tell Your story. The story of how You took me deeper and higher and further with You than I ever thought possible.*

At the end of Job's struggle with the Lord, he said, "I had heard of you by the hearing of the ear, but now my eye sees you" (Job 42:5).

Through suffering, Job learned. He grew. He saw God in a new way, the way of reverence and awe. When we come face to face with the power of the One who created all things and through whom all have their life and breath and being, we begin to see things as they really are, not through those rose-colored glasses I threw away long ago.

Truth. That's what I wanted. That's what I got. That's what I have to tell.

God has always taught us through stories, through the lives of ordinary human beings. Here's mine. It isn't tidy or fun or sweet or cute. But it's mine, and it's Bronner's. Someone might say he "died" for this story. I hope it will mean something to you.

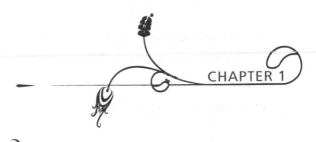

A CROWN OF GREAT WORTH

Friday, September 18, 2009

I've been thinking about the word *pool* and the images it evokes.

Say it out loud.

"Pool."

Sounds very pleasant, doesn't it? Kind of makes me think of blue birds bathing in a birdbath with Snow White singing in the background. *Pool of water.* Cool, refreshing, crisp, easy . . . a summer day spent in play . . . lazy laughter . . . splashing . . . children. And what about water itself? Life-sustaining water.

An ice cold drink on a hot day, cleansing showers, large bodies of water with ships anchored offshore, waves crashing along the beach, beautiful bays and coves filled with fish. . . .

I think of the sea lions sunbathing on the rocks in Baja, sailboats gently moving along with the breeze, a catamaran ride at Martha's Vineyard, the fishing pond down at our farm in Jemison, and I think of heaven where the River of Life flows through and where my baby lives.

I have a pool in my backyard, and it is lovely. It was designed for us by a friend and has lush trees and plantings all around. Just yesterday, I went down by the pool and clipped a couple of flowers to put in a vase for my table. I go outside and stare at it so many days, and then I leave to go sit by Bronner's grave and pray and hope and long for him and the place where he is and the Person he is with.

I never really thought about our separation from God's physical presence until I was separated from a person I know and love more than life itself, and no matter how hard I reach for him, I can't get to him. I can't be where he is—not now, not yet.

When Bronner drowned in that lovely pool that isn't so lovely to me anymore—even if the mourning doves bathe in it in the morning and the dragonflies drop in for a drink in summer and bumblebees swarm around the blooms of the chastity trees—I realized that I may be separated from the one thing in life I enjoyed the most at the time for a long time: my beautiful, precious, dear child. And, it made me see that, although God's Spirit lives within me, I can't *see* Him. I can't *touch* Him. I can't *be* where Jesus is, not now, not yet.

Jesus lives in heaven, in paradise, where there in the midst of the Garden still stands the Tree of Life (Revelation 2:7), and I live on the earth, a fallen and cursed world where light and darkness live together, where every night we are reminded of death, but each morning are given the gift of a new hope, a second chance to live. Here on the earth, the changing leaves of autumn ring in the cold, still sleep of winter, but in the springtime, an awakening occurs that lasts through summer sunshine until . . . a new fall begins.

Bronner's spirit is still with me: I have memories of him. I know him and I love him. I know where he is and imagine what he might be doing, but I can't hold him. My eyes have pictures and videos of Bronner to look at, but my arms are empty of him. He would be four years old now, as I write this chapter, and I know he would be different. I know he would be bigger and would have a lot more to say. He would be in Mrs. Darden's 4K class this year. But I don't get to be her room mom or have the class over for a Charlie Brown Christmas party like I did for my other two boys who had her. I don't get to go on Bronner's very first field trip to Bud's Best Cookies or to any of them, for that matter, the Old Baker Farm, the Golden Flake Company, or even the Caldwell Mill Animal Clinic right down from our house. I don't get to do any of that, nor do I get to watch him get out of the car in the mornings at carpool or wave good-bye to him and say, "I love you."

Sometimes, I can still pick up the scent of him in his room. I go there and sit in the glider where I rocked him and sang to him and felt the warmth of him lying on my chest snuggled up underneath his baby blanket. Rick and I have both, on separate occasions, and not just once or twice either, gone into his room and read to ourselves one of his favorite books, *Cowboy Small*. His room is decorated in a Western theme. Still hanging on his wall by a nail and some rope is a cute little painted board that says, "Goodnight, little cowboy, close your eyes and dream." It's hung over the side of his crib where his stuffed "Moo-moo" still lies as if waiting to be held again by its owner. Bronner used Moo-moo as a pillow until it was replaced by an oversized LarryBoy, his favorite *VeggieTales* character. He carried "Larry" around everywhere he went, even though Larry was as big as he.

His Larry was buried with him, and I have hoped that Bronner has it in heaven. The director of preschool ministries at our church, Brenda Clark, had a mural of Jesus surrounded by children painted on the preschool floor. Bronner is there holding his Larry, just as I envision him to be, at times, in his little blue boots, red shirt, and jeans. So now only Moo-moo remains, and Bronner's mommy and daddy pick him up sometimes and breathe in as deeply as we can, searching for just a hint of a certain smell that was distinctly Bronner's own. Most of his other toys and clothes and blankets and things are still there in his room, too. Some people might say that's selfish of me to keep them, but I don't care. I can't take them out, not now, not yet. They're his things, and every time I walk in there and see them, I can somehow see him. He's not there any more than he's in the grave I sit by, but all of it seems to help me to remember that once, not so long ago, I held in my arms a baby boy with golden hair and sunshine in his eyes.

The thing I miss the most, I think, is his smile. It was a smile that wasn't just given with one part of him, but with all of him, a whole-self smile—the kind that grabs you and wraps you all up inside of it so that you can't help but to return it in the exact same way, with a whole-self smile right back. That's how Bronner made me feel always, like I was smiling with a whole-self smile all the time. He smiled every time he saw me. Every time. I remember one day when I was picking him up from Mother's Day Out, quietly enjoying watching him play until finally he looked up and saw me. He yelled, "Mommy!" so big and so loud with the kind of excitement you'd expect if I'd been gone for half a year instead of half a day. Then, he ran over to me and jumped up in my arms, and I squeezed him and kissed that soft cheek of his so many times as I greeted him in my little baby voice that all the older kids loved to hear me do. I got his bag and said good-bye to his teachers, who were loving every minute of this sweet reunion of mommy and child—after only being gone from each other for a few hours of time. And I beamed from way down deep inside with such love and joy and happiness and pride in this, my most beautiful child, my baby, my Bronner.

Of all the people in the world, he was mine! He was mine! That face of his, that spunk, that giggle, that exuberant personality, that favorite child of everyone who knew him, that sweet friend and grandchild, the one Lindsey babysat on some Saturday nights. She loved him so much. She said she wanted to name her own baby after him when she had one, and her sisters say they're going to name their babies after my other two they babysat for, Brooks and Brody.

My housekeeper, Cynthia, who kept Bronner for me sometimes if I was running errands that morning or going up to the school or for a run, loved him, too. She remembers him and mourns for him. She still comes to our house sometimes to clean, but she doesn't have to wash any clothes in gentle detergent anymore or make sure there are clean sippy cups in the cupboard. She'll never have to make him Cream of Wheat for me again, but she remembers, as I remember, the night she and her husband took him shopping with them while I was getting prepared for Christmas. She told me she didn't correct the woman who said, "Oh, what a beautiful boy you have!" She took the compliment with pride because in a way he did belong to her. He belonged to her and to Dr. Larusso, who was treating his allergy to ant bites. (By the way, I don't think there are any ants in heaven, and that's why Bronner was so allergic to them. He wasn't going to be where they were very long and would have no reason to have immunity to them. But if, by chance, they are there, then they most certainly do not bite little boys.)

Bronner belonged to his Pop, a retired football coach, who could already see his robust, husky grandson out on the football field. He belonged to his Daddy, who couldn't wait to see him in

> It's a harsh reality, a very severe punishment that makes us see how God really feels about sin. He hates it and doles out very harsh punishment for it. Death.

his first T-ball uniform, and who, like me, beamed with pride at the sight of him.

He belonged to Miss Patty, who was more than happy to hold that sweet baby on her chest and rock him to sleep that day when I was running late to pick him up from Mother's Day Out. He belonged to Miss Jeannie, who kept him and lots of his friends at her house some mornings in the summer. I have a picture in my bedroom of him there. He's sitting on a log, wearing his swimsuit, and eating a sucker. It reminds me of a most beautiful summer—the best summer—the summer when I still had Bronner.

He belonged to Marie, who cut his hair, and to his Nana, who held him as he broke out in hives from an ant bite one day. She remembers how he was patting her with his strong baby arms as he held onto her. Bronner was his Maw-Maw's, who couldn't be with him very often but had his picture displayed so prominently for everyone to see and who got the special privilege of holding him the day he left the earth for heaven. And Bronner was his Memaw's, Rick's grandmother, who, after Bronner left this world, soon followed suit.

He belonged to Blake, who ran with him on the football field after his games were over every Friday night in the fall and who threw him up in the air and held him so high, and to Brandi who said he was cutest one of them all—her brothers. He belonged to Brooks and Brody, who played "busy bee" with him on their way to school, who held him when he was first born, and watched him grow into the boy who played "crash" with them and loved *Bible Man* and *VeggieTales* and to run and to play in the sand and to slide and to hit baseballs off a tee.

So many things, so many people, so many memories. Bronner belonged to us all back then, but now he belongs to heaven. And all of us, everyone who knew him and loved him, see things so differently now. The world isn't what we thought it was. The baby his daddy called "Cornbread" on the radio is gone from it. We expect people who are old and who have lived their lives to die. We expect and sometimes are even glad when someone who is suffering with disease and pain gets to go on to heaven. But when someone like Bronner, who in our eyes was perfect in every way, goes away up yonder, it's just so wrong, so unexpected, a slap in the face. It's a reality check for us all that this world is no good. God said it was very good after He created it, but it's not good anymore. It's cursed. It's cursed by God Himself. He cursed it and punished all of creation because of sin.

It's a very severe punishment: death. Death *shouldn't be*, but it *is*. We were never meant to be separated from the ones we love. Our spirits were not made to live outside of our bodies. But God formed Adam's body out of the dust of the earth, and then He blew some of His life-giving Spirit into the body He had created for the Spirit. They belong together, body and spirit, and when a spirit is ripped from its body, it tears. This isn't an easy thing. It's not a pretty thing. It's so unnatural. We think death is just a part of life, but it shouldn't be. Do we get that?

It shouldn't be. It's a harsh reality, a very severe punishment that makes us see how God really feels about sin. He hates it and doles out very harsh punishment for it. Death.

> The LORD God took the man and put him in the garden of Eden to work it and keep it. And the LORD God commanded the man, saying, "You may surely eat of every tree of the garden, but of the tree of the knowledge of good and evil you shall not eat, for in the day that you eat of it you shall surely die."
>
> —GENESIS 2:15–17, AUTHOR'S EMPHASIS

When I found my baby floating in the pool in our backyard, I rushed to get him and ran inside and laid him on the couch and tried to breathe air into his lungs. And there I beheld . . . my baby, the one I had just held moments before and was showing the snow that had fallen that day in Birmingham. The one I had loved and cherished and prayed and fasted for, the one I wanted. When I saw him lying there without his spirit in his little baby body, it wasn't right. It was wrong. It was so unnatural. It wasn't supposed to be.

Pools of water aren't supposed to steal, kill, and destroy. They're supposed to be fun!

Don't you remember when you were a kid? Pools were fun! And it was a special privilege to ever get to swim in one. I felt like a princess when I was a little girl and got to go to my aunt's house that had a pool. Me and my brothers and my cousins, we swam and ate popsicles and had sandwiches for lunch. It was a beautiful day.

I wanted Bronner to have beautiful days—every day.

I wanted my children to look back on their childhood with fondness, not heartbreak! My boys, Brooks and Brody, and my stepchildren, Brandi and Blake . . . they know what heartbreak is, no matter how hard I tried to shield them from it. My plans for them weren't God's plans for them. My dreams were only dreams, but God knew the truth, the reality. God knew what was to be. He knew what was coming. He had prepared it in advance, far in advance, before the world began, the work that He was to give Bronner, and the work that He would carry on to completion through Rick and through me and through our remaining children. He tried to prepare us for what was coming, but we didn't listen. We couldn't see.

We couldn't see that life here on earth can't be manipulated into perfection. This world isn't heaven, no matter how hard I tried to make it that. I had wanted my children to have everything I didn't have as a child. I had envisioned their childhood to be full and rich and joyful. Rick and I would take them on trips to Walt Disney World and to the beach. They would live in a beautiful home and have nice clothes to wear and lots of toys

Everything could be beautiful now. God had something different in mind.

to play with. Their backyard would be a literal playground, and I would give them all of me. I wouldn't work outside the home. I would make their childhood magical with whopping Santa visits and Easter baskets filled to overflowing. They would be good at sports and go to the best colleges and universities. When I was pregnant with Brooks, I even had thoughts of Harvard for him. Of course, my kids would get a sound Christian education. They would grow up in one church, going every Sunday, and I would teach their Sunday School classes.

And it was like that for a while. Our life as a family was beautiful. It wasn't perfect, but we were happy. Our life was full. It was loud. It had the pitter-patter of small feet running through its hallways and silly giggles after snuggling up together all in one bed on Saturday mornings . . . three little boys, two teenagers, Rick, and me. (Well, the teenagers usually slept in on Saturday mornings, but we were always together for Sunday lunch.) "Table for seven, please." Oh, how I miss that! It was kind of crazy for us to think it was even possible, going out to eat after church, the seven of us, but it didn't stop us from trying. So many times, there we were sitting in a too-small booth with Bronner being restless and wanting to get down and run around and not wanting to wait on his meal. He was usually at the end of his rope by the time we got our food and was having to be carried around the restaurant or taken outside because he was so loud.

It was always a big mess, but it was crazy fun! We were Burgesses. The boys were big, the laughter intense, and the love very real.

Our family might have been messy, but we were very happy and filled with much love for one another. We were seeking the Lord and growing step by step by step with each trial, each difficulty, and even each joy teaching us something new of the Lord. I thought I knew God and His ways, but God was about to show me something very different from what I had seen of Him before. He had blessed me with a husband who loved and cherished me. He had given me my heart's desire—children—some I had given birth to and some I had not, three who lived with me all the time, and two I saw at breaks and starts (or, to put it in common terms, every other weekend and on holidays and vacations), but mine just the same. Shared children have your heart in a strange way, by the way. You have to let go of them sometimes in order to not despair at their absence but then open your heart back up as wide as you can on their return. I couldn't even imagine their other life with their mom and stepdad. Their life with me was all I knew and really all I wanted to know. In my heart, they were mine even if I did have to give them up so often.

I know I lived in somewhat of a fantasy world where everything was lovely and grand, kind of like what I had imagined life was like for Elizabeth Bennet after she married Mr. Darcy in Jane Austen's novel, *Pride and Prejudice*. I clearly had messed up in my youth, but I had found my prince, and the long lost Father I never really had walked with as a child. Everything could be beautiful now.

God had something different in mind.

My plans were plans made foolishly, by someone who had no idea what the future held for those children, someone who couldn't see, someone not completely blind but absolutely too worldly, someone who cared way too much about what she could give to her children. Sure, God was among those many things I had envisioned for them. They were going to have the best of God *and* the best of the world. Their childhood would be . . . well . . . heavenly.

What I've had to learn is that, although God gave me my children to enjoy the blessings of and to learn from them, He has plans for them *I know nothing about.* My children didn't and don't belong to me. God created them, and He has a unique calling on each of their lives. I now know that they weren't given life just to have fun, but they were given life in order to seek out and find God, to glorify Him, and to be used for His purposes and His kingdom forever.

They were created for relationship with God.

This teaching began long before Bronner was born. It began, I think, in the pastor's office of our old church in Oxford, Alabama, where Rick and I spent the first two years of our marriage. We were moving and had come to say good-bye to the man who had become a father figure to us both. As we were leaving, Brother Jerry asked if he could pray for us and wanted to know if there was anything we specifically wanted him to pray for. Without even a pause, I spoke up. "Please pray that I can stay home with my baby and not have to work outside the home when I have him." It would be my first baby, Brooks. And he did.

Of all the things I could have asked this righteous man to pray for, I asked him to pray that I would be able to stay home and not work, for Rick to be able to provide for us without my working outside the home. I wanted to be a stay-at-home mom because I wanted to be able to relish in my children's babyhood. We were yet to learn that what we want isn't always what we need.

I could have asked Brother Jerry to pray that Brooks would be healthy, that he would grow to love the Lord and come to salvation early so that he wouldn't have to look back at his life with regret when he is old, or that God would shield him from heartbreak.

I could have asked Brother Jerry to pray for so many things, but I didn't. I basically asked for money: a stupid, flippant, careless request because it wasn't about Brooks, really. It was about me and the fun I wanted to have with him. See how selfish and worldly I was? God had to change that woman.

God granted the request. He doubled, maybe even tripled, Rick's salary in my eighth month of pregnancy with Brooks. I did get to stay home with him, and I did relish in his babyhood. But it wasn't what I expected. It even started off badly in the hospital with a placental abruption that could have killed him. Rick says that as they were rushing me down the hallway for an emergency C-section, he asked what he could do. The answer was emphatic. "Pray!"

Rick did pray. He prayed for our lives because the baby and I were both in trouble. Within minutes, the doctor held Brooks up for Rick to see and gave him the thumbs-up. Then he pointed to me and gave another thumbs-up. Rick breathed a sigh of relief, just for a moment, and then he heard a still, small voice within his spirit saying, *What if they hadn't been OK? What if I had taken them? Would I have been any less great to you?*

See, God was preparing us by giving us lesser trials, pains, and struggles in order to get us ready for the big one—the unthinkable, the unbelievable, the thing that makes men realize how stupid and petty and sinful and silly we really can be. We don't know anything except what God reveals to us. We are nothing but dust, and our lives are just a vapor, a mist that will be gone very soon. We think we are so wise, but we don't know anything. We can't know that our baby will drown at two-and-a-half years old.

Bronner's hand slips softly out of mine, and I walk into the warm embrace of a Father.

We don't expect things like that. We couldn't even go there in our minds. The joy we feel when we bring our precious babies home from the hospital is the only thing we can really know here on earth. But God knew. He knew what was coming. I didn't know, but God knew.

He, Himself, allowed it because He knew He could use it to bring glory to His name and to His kingdom, to bring lost souls to Himself, and to refine a couple of Christians who were too caught up in the things of this world. He crushed them. He crushed us, Rick and me, into fine powder and let Satan sift us like wheat to be blown away with the wind. But with His breath, God caught that wind and began building something else, something different. He took that dust that was Rick and Sherri Burgess and added a little of His living water and built us again, not with flesh and blood, but with His own Spirit.

But sometimes, when I'm sitting on the couch next to Rick or riding along in the van with him, I remember how Bronner felt when I would hold him. I can almost feel again the weight of a two-and-a-half-year-old lying on my chest. I remember playing peekaboo, hiding under the covers in my bed, with him just giggling. He loved it. He was filled with joy, and he filled my days with joy. I was so happy, so very happy. And although I know and feel and love and cherish him still, I'm not with him. I'm not where he is, and I am not where God is.

I know all about God. I have felt His presence, and I have heard His voice speaking to my spirit. But I can't behold Him as the Apostle John did. I can't tell you by firsthand experience what He looks like. I can only tell you what I've read and seen in paintings. I can tell you what Bronner looks like because I have that firsthand knowledge of Bronner, but I wasn't here to see Jesus when He walked on the earth. I've never had the great honor of seeing the glorified Christ as the Apostles Peter, James, John, and Paul did, nor have I gazed upon His *shekinah* ("dwelling") glory as so many did in Old Testament days. Oh, how I long for the day when I can!

I can only imagine. I imagine this glorious reunion with Bronner in heaven:

> As soon as I walk through those gates, he'll run to me and yell out with glee, "Mommy!" He'll jump up into my arms, and I'll hold him and cry and laugh at the same time for a very long time. I'll snuggle him so close to me, we'll be like one person and not two, and I'll kiss his very soft cheek a thousand times before I put him down again. And then he'll take me by the hand and lead me around heaven, showing me the place he's been all this time and telling me how he's been spending his days. He'll show me splendor and gloriously beautiful things beyond all comparison. And I will be awestruck and elated and happy once again. But this time, I will also be holy, pure, away from anything that hinders, away from anything dark. This is the kingdom of light, and Bronner and I are both glowing in and with that light.
>
> I see a sparkling river and flowers and trees and animals. But I'm not afraid. The lions here aren't fearsome, and dogs don't snarl. Mosquitoes don't bite, and flies do not swarm. I don't have to check Bronner for ticks after a visit with the farm animals and a run through the hayfield. It's so lovely, so beautiful, and the culmination of it all is when Bronner leads me home, my heart's home, to my Friend, my Brother, my Lord, and my Savior. Bronner's hand slips softly out of mine, and I walk into the warm embrace of a Father. I melt into Him, and we are no longer

two people, but one. And I cry and I laugh and rest there for a very long time. His face says it all. He doesn't have to say anything. It's radiant but kind and gentle and filled with empathy and love for me. And then, earth will fade away as a distant memory, like a dream, a bad dream, and heaven becomes my new reality. Heaven is my home now, and Jesus Himself wipes away all of my tears.

John saw Jesus standing beside the throne of God dressed in priestly robes with a golden sash, eyes blazing with fire, and feet shining like burnished bronze refined in a furnace. He spoke these words in a voice like the roar of many waters, "Do not be afraid. I am the First and the Last. I am the Living One; I was dead, and now look, I am alive forever and ever! And I hold the keys of death and Hades" (Revelation 1:17–18 NIV). That gives me unspeakable comfort, knowing that the First and the Last, the Living One, the One who holds the keys of death and Hades, is on my side. He calls me *friend* and *sister* and *child*. He loves me and cherishes me the way I cherish my own sweet babies.

He's taken me by the hand and hasn't left me for one second during this very hard time of testing. He's leading me by the hand, right now, down very treacherous slopes and over very turbulent seas. This isn't where He leads me beside the still waters or makes me to lie down in green pastures. No, but even though I walk through the valley of the shadow of death, I will fear no evil, because look who's holding my hand! The Living One, the Alpha and the Omega, the One with the name above every other name, the One who is above all things . . . not the least of which is death. He's holding the keys of death and Hades, and I belong to Him! I belong to the King. He has marked me with a seal and has called me His own, so I will not fear. I will not turn back. I will mount up with wings like eagles with renewed strength and vigor. I will walk and not faint, and I will run and not grow weary. I will endure this pain, the heartbreak, the suffering. And in the end I will win, if I do not give up, the crown of righteousness and gain eternal life.

What is not worth that?

I want the glorious reunion with Bronner and the sweet embrace of my heavenly Father, so I wait. I am learning to be patient and to stand, not by my own strength or in my own will, but all through Him who leads me by the hand, the One who loves me and never forsakes me, the Living One, the Alpha and the Omega, the First and the Last.

HEARTS MADE READY

I see parents of young children around town all the time now — at ballgames, at the grocery store, at school — and every time I see a parent walking along with one of those precious toddlers like Bronner was, they're smiling. Every time. They're so happy and proud and content because they have a sweet, adorable, and cherished treasure in their midst. It doesn't happen with older kids so much maybe because all of that joy begins to mix in with the trials and pain that life in this world inevitably brings to the equation. But with the babies, the toddlers, it always does. I remember that happiness.

I was so happy just to be with Bronner. I loved to just look at him, to hold him, to kiss him, to feed him, to bathe him, even to change his diaper. I loved every minute with him. He was just fun, a big ball of beautiful, soft, and cozy fun, like a cookie right out of the oven, so warm and toasty and good.

Every morning was like Christmas morning with him. Every morning I would bounce up the stairs, barely able to wait until I could pick him up out of his crib and snuggle him close to me. He would carry his "Larry" with him down the stairs, lay his head on my shoulder, and stick that thumb in his mouth. (Don't picture

"Larry" as just a small stuffed toy. Bronner's "Larry" had been part of a book display that wasn't something you could buy in stores. It was more like a big pillow. Rick had talked the *VeggieTales* people into letting him have it at an event they were both involved in.) It was a big bundle of joy I was carrying around with me, and I loved it!

We would pause midway down the stairs to look out the window at what Bronner called "a squir." He hadn't yet learned how to say the whole word, *squirrel*, but he loved them. Brody created "the squirrel club" for himself, his daddy, and Bronner to be in. Brooks thought he was too old to be in the squirrel club. He liked to bounce and swing on his pogo instead. But Brody and Bronner would run around at the bottom of the yard and sword fight with sticks and fall down on the ground and roll around. Sometimes, we would look for fireflies, or lightening bugs as we called them when I was girl. We'd put them in jars and watch them light up.

Bronner loved "outside." He would go to the door and say, "Outside, outside."

One day, we were outside at Veteran's Park, where we walked around the lake together, and *this time* he really did walk because of the gravel he wanted to lie down and roll around in and scoop up handfuls of to throw in the water. Then, when he got so tired, I jumped up in the swing and pulled him in close to me and sang, "Baby mine, don't you cry. Baby mine, dry your eyes. Let your eyes sparkle and shine, never a tear, baby of mine . . . Baby mine, don't you cry. Baby mine, dry your eyes. Rest your head close to my heart, never to part. Baby of mine."

Bronner liked for me to sing to him. He would point to me and say, "Sing!" And I would. I used to sing to him, "You are my sunshine, my only sunshine. You make me happy when skies are gray. You'll never know, dear, how much I love you. Please don't take my Bronner away." But, God did. He did take my Bronner away.

Sometimes, I think God gave me all those wonderful moments with Bronner to look back on and to remember that He had been good to me. He gave me a glimpse, a glimmer of heaven in that time to look back on as proof of His love and grace toward me so it could carry me through the cold, dark night that lay unsuspecting just around the bend.

I guess there were hints that it was coming, but we never think it's going to be the baby, do we?

When Samuel came to Jesse to appoint one of his sons as king over Israel, Jesse didn't even show him the baby of the family. David was left outside tending the sheep.

Jesse sent seven sons to Samuel before the prophet finally had to ask, "Are all your sons here?"

"For the LORD sees not as man sees: man looks on the outward appearance, but the LORD looks on the heart" (1 Samuel 16:7).

I can attest to the fact that Bronner had a heart of gold, even at two and a half. He had been raised in a Christian home, and he knew who Jesus was. He sang, "Jesus loves me, this I know." He bowed his head for prayer. He had been protected from evil, shielded from the world, and he was pure, innocent, ready . . . ready at two and a half . . . for heaven. Not that all two-and-a-half-year-old boys aren't ready. It was just Bronner's time. He was living out his purpose. God chose him for this. God created him for this. God also knew my heart and Rick's heart and how we would respond to having our sunshine baby taken up into the clouds without us.

"And some of them also I will take for priests and for Levites, says the LORD" (Isaiah 66:21).

But, in my mind at the time, Brooks was the one set aside for the Lord's service. Brody was his helper. And, Bronner . . . Bronner was my reward for all the hard-fought battles I had already won concerning my children. He was going to be a crowning joy for me, and maybe when everything is said and done, I will find that I was right, that he had been my reward all along. He is my heavenly treasure waiting for me, preserved for me. Am I rejoicing over this yet? Probably not. But I know that I will someday because I believe that even in this I have passed the test.

> *Blessed be the God and Father of our Lord Jesus Christ! According to his great mercy, he has caused us to be born again to a living hope through the resurrection of Jesus Christ from the dead, to an inheritance that is imperishable, undefiled, and unfading, kept in heaven for you, who by God's power are being guarded through faith for a salvation ready to be revealed in the last time. In this you rejoice, though now for a little while, if necessary, you have been grieved by various trials, so that the tested genuineness of your faith — more precious than gold that perishes though it is tested by fire — may be found to result in praise and glory and honor at the revelation of Jesus Christ. Though you have not seen him, you love him. Though you do not now see him, you believe in him and rejoice with joy that is inexpressible and filled with glory, obtaining the outcome of your faith, the salvation of your souls.*
>
> —1 PETER 1:3–9

Brody is four years and four days older than Bronner, so when I was pregnant with Bronner, Brody was still really just a baby. And, oh, was he the most beautiful thing inside and out. He reminded me of David, a precious, pure, handsome little guy. Brody is the only one of our sons who has his daddy's dark skin. The other three are fairer. He also has large, almond-shaped eyes that are a color all their own, not completely brown like Brandi and Brooks have, but certainly not blue like mine. It all reminded me of 1 Samuel 16:12, "Now he was ruddy and had beautiful eyes and was handsome. And the LORD said, 'Arise, anoint him, for this is he.'"

I was a core group leader that year (2004–2005) at Community Bible Study, and we were studying 1 and 2 Corinthians, which as you may know, speak of God as the "Father of mercies and God of all comfort" (2 Corinthians 1:3). This brought up the fact that there was a woman in my group who'd had a child already go to heaven. She spoke about it in detail, scaring me to death! I had two stepchildren and two precious little boys, and I was very pregnant with another baby boy. To have a child's life taken from her is every mother's worst nightmare. But this woman had lived through it and was right there telling us about it.

It had been her only child, a daughter she had raised almost to adulthood. Her daughter was in college when an undiagnosed aneurism burst, killing her almost instantly. Sudden calamity, sudden horror that no one was expecting or looking for.

I began to worry that I might lose a child, and specifically Brody. I remember sharing my anxieties with my core group one Thursday, to the point of tears. The fear was real, especially on that day. Rick and I had decided that before Bronner was born we would give each of the other children a special trip. We knew from experience that once a new baby comes home, he would take up lots of our time and attention, so we wanted to make sure that each of the other children felt as special as we knew this new baby was going to be. I had already taken Brandi to New York City for her

For that day *is* coming when no one will ever bear a child for calamity, or for "sudden terror," as my Bible's footnote clarifies for me.

birthday in December, as she is such the theater buff. Rick's mother and sister went with us, too, so it was kind of a girl's trip. And Rick had already taken the oldest two boys to Universal Studios in Orlando, since they both love roller coasters and music. Although Blake and Brooks are separated by eight years, their birthdays are close to each other on the calendar. Brooks was born February 7 and Blake's birthday is one month and one day later, on March 8. So they went together for their trip, stayed at the Hard Rock Hotel, and had an absolute blast. Now for the little one's turn. Brody and his daddy were leaving that day for Walt Disney World on a special trip for just the two of them.

Brody was in a class at Community Bible Study with me, and he and I were going to meet Rick at the airport after it was over that day. I was so afraid something was going to happen to Brody on that trip. I didn't know what, but I was terrified until . . . I went to his classroom to pick him up. He was wearing a little necklace they had made with yarn and construction paper. It simply said, "I will keep you in all places" (Genesis 28:15, paraphrase).

That's all it took, and I believed. I believed that God had given me a message that day and placed it around Brody's little neck. (We still have that necklace, by the way.) The Holy Spirit used the Word to prompt a spirit of peace about Brody's safety. As God had promised Jacob in the Bible, I felt His assurance: "I have him in my hand, and no harm will befall him" (Genesis 28:15, paraphrase). I was at complete peace with Brody going with his dad after that. I knew God to be faithful. I knew He would watch over my baby and keep him safe.

The foreboding feeling wasn't for nothing, though. One of my children would be taken from me. It just wouldn't be the one I had feared.

I had forgotten or hadn't made the connection between myself and Hannah and Bronner and Samuel. I had tried and tried to get pregnant with him, but it just wasn't happening. I was getting older, and with each child it had gotten harder. For Brooks, it was a couple of months until I had a plus sign. For Brody, it took six months. For Bronner, it took us a year.

But there's so much more to it than that. I wanted a girl, a little girl who would live with me all the time and that I didn't have to miss the baby years with. I wanted a baby girl who looked like me. Brandi stopped looking like a daughter of mine at about age 12 when she became six inches taller than me. Everyone thought we were sisters, even when I was in my thirties and she was in her teens! It was ridiculous. I thought, "Do people not see my wrinkles? Just because I'm five feet and one inch tall doesn't mean I'm 15 years old!" (OK, so now Brandi is five feet eleven inches tall, by the way—ten inches taller than me! But sadly, it's becoming more and more evident that I'm the older one.)

Anyway, we even got the stupid book on how to determine the sex of your baby and tried all that timing it out . . . yada, yada, yada. Nothing. So we threw the book out and just tried for anything. Still nothing. And I was going back and forth with whether or not to even have another baby. Maybe the four we already had were enough, so I prayed to God for it to be His will. "I can't decide this, Lord. You decide. But just tell me so I'll know." Every month, the same thing over and over and over again, the disappointment of yet another negative pregnancy test. I got 11 months' worth of minus signs before my something really positive happened.

About that time, my current pastor, Dr. Danny Wood, preached a sermon on fasting. He laid it all out for us and told us exactly what to do and why. The "why" was what caught my attention. He told us that he had once fasted to receive an answer from the Lord on whether to continue as our pastor. He had fasted for 40 days in 2001, only consuming what he and his wife, Janice, juiced from whole fruits and vegetables, along with an occasional broth. God not only affirmed that he should remain but that he should lead an initiative to take us, as a church, on mission into every time zone in the world within the decade. He called it the 2010 Vision.

I took copious notes that day: "Fasting is abstaining from food or an activity so that we may completely focus on the Lord."

From Danny's "Expected Results of a Fast," here's what really stood out to me: *clearer direction for the next step.*

That's what I needed, all right! Pastor Danny had gotten an answer to his big question. It was "yes," thankfully! So, I began to pray about whether or not I should fast to receive an answer to my big question. I remember that time in my walk with God and how I had asked Him to help me to crucify the sin in my life, not just to get rid of it on a temporary basis but to kill it, to crucify it based on Galatians 5:24, which says, "And those who belong to Christ Jesus have crucified the flesh with its passions and desires."

Danny's sermon was given on Sunday, September 26, 2004.

I have kept a prayer journal for years, and the prayer I prayed on Monday, September 27, 2004, begins like this:

> Father God, make me holy like You. Sanctify me by the truth. Make me glorify You in all my words, deeds, and actions. Set me on a course to crucify the sin in my life. I know that Your Holy Spirit has empowered me to resist sin. I pray for protection from the evil one. And I thank

You for choosing me and setting me apart for Your good purposes. Help me to discover how You want to use me . . .

People always say to be careful what you pray for. I prayed for God to "crucify the sin in my life." He heard me. I was about to be crucified with Christ, and yet I would live.

That week, I decided that "yes," fasting was what I needed to do in order to receive an answer on whether the Lord wanted me to have another baby. I went out and bought a juicer and some fresh fruits and vegetables, and by that Friday, I was ready to begin my fast. I started fasting and praying for a baby according to God's will on October 1, 2004. I had an answer the very next day!

We were celebrating Rick's fortieth birthday that night with a party I was throwing for him. When I was getting ready for the party, I noticed a bump. At that time I was thin enough that if I'd had nothing but fruit juices for a day and a half, my tummy should have been flat. But it wasn't. There was just a slight little bump there. When I noticed it, I took out a pregnancy test—I had plenty of them on hand from all that trying we had been going back and forth about—took it, and finally got that plus sign I had been looking for.

Hey, Danny! I got a "yes," too! I was so excited!

Of course, I must have already been pregnant when I decided to do that fast, and even when I prayed for the Lord to set me on a path to crucify the sin in my life, but I didn't know that. The Lord, however, did know. Bronner was going to be the answer to *all* my prayers—the elation and happiness, the pain and the purpose, the crucifixion, the growth, everything . . . all wrapped up in one little bundle of joy. God knew this. It had been His plan all along, in His perfect timing. He had just been waiting for me—for me to be ready for it, for me to pray for it, for me to ask for it and to fast for it. He had been waiting on my obedience, for me to be able to hear Him speak. I really had been growing in the Lord that year. I was in Community Bible Study, as I've said, but I was also doing a lot of other reading. And I was learning . . . a lot.

> *But do not overlook this one fact, beloved, that with the Lord one day is as a thousand years, and a thousand years as one day. The Lord is not slow to fulfill his promise as some count slowness, but is patient toward you, not wishing that any should perish, but that all should reach repentance.*
>
> —2 PETER 3:8–9

I decided I would go ahead and make the announcement that night at the party. We were so happy! I don't think it's a coincidence that Rick was turning 40, either. Forty is the number of probation in the Bible. We know this from examples such as the rain of the flood lasting for 40 days and 40 nights, the wandering of the Israelites in the wilderness for 40 years before being allowed into their Promised Land, the fact that Nineveh was given 40 days to repent, and because Jesus Himself had been tempted by the devil for 40 days.

Rick and I had stood our ground for God in many things, but after this fortieth year for my husband, God would give him the Abraham test: "Will you accept that I am asking for a son from you?"

This would be the son I had prayed and fasted for as Hannah had prayed and fasted for Samuel. And, as she had to give her son back to the Lord, so would I, and at about the same age, too. The Bible tells us that when Hannah had weaned Samuel, she brought him to the temple to live and to serve there for God, and we know that in Bible times, women nursed their babies for about two and a half years.

Hannah said to her husband Elkanah, "As soon as the child is weaned, I will bring him, so that he may appear in the presence of the LORD and dwell there forever" (1 Samuel 1:22). Elkanah agreed to that, and when she did bring him up before Eli, the priest, she said, "For this child I prayed, and the LORD has granted me my petition that I made to him. Therefore I have lent him to the LORD" (vv. 27–28).

I am certain of this one thing: I, too, have only "lent" my son to the Lord as Hannah did. Psalm 127:3 tells us, "Children are a heritage from the LORD, the fruit of the womb a reward." Bronner was and is my heritage, my reward, and I know the Lord has only taken him away for a time . . . a short time . . . and that soon and very soon, I *will* see him again. I will take him into my arms and hold him again like I've never held him before . . . in perfection . . . in peace . . . in holiness . . . and without *any* fear.

For that day *is* coming when no one will ever bear a child for calamity, or for "sudden terror," as my Bible's footnote clarifies for me.

> *"For behold, I create new heavens and a new earth, and the former things shall not be remembered or come into mind. But be glad and rejoice forever in that which I create; for behold, I create Jerusalem to be a joy, and her people to be a gladness. I will rejoice in Jerusalem and be glad in my people; no more shall be heard in it the sound of weeping and the cry of distress. No more shall there be in it an infant who lives but a few days, or an old man who does not fill out his days, for the young man shall die a hundred years old, and the sinner a hundred years old shall be accursed. They shall build houses and inhabit them; they shall plant vineyards and eat their fruit. They*

*shall not build and another inhabit; they shall not plant
and another eat; for like the days of a tree shall the days of
my people be, and my chosen shall long enjoy the work of
their hands. They shall not labor in vain or bear children
for calamity, for they shall be the offspring of the blessed
of the LORD, and their descendants with them. Before they
call I will answer; while they are yet speaking I will hear.
The wolf and the lamb shall graze together; the lion shall
eat straw like the ox, and dust shall be the serpent's food.
They shall not hurt or destroy in all my holy mountain,"
says the LORD.*

—ISAIAH 65:17–25

When I was pregnant with Bronner, I have mentioned that I took Brandi to New York for her birthday. Something happened on that trip that made the truth of the gospel come alive for me. We weren't too far removed from 9/11, so three women and a teenage girl getting into the car with someone who was obviously of the Muslim faith was still a little scary in December 2004. I remember pausing for only a moment before jumping into the front seat of that taxicab. Nana, Sissy, and Brandi rode in the backseat and didn't say a word the whole time. It was a long ride, too, because we were going to the airport. It was also morning, so the traffic was kind of bad. It gave us a lot of time to talk.

I sent an email to my pastor about the conversation I had with my taxi driver and the insights I received because of it. Pastor Danny was now leading our church on a journey into missions that was intense, pervasive, and high priority, and I wanted to encourage him with what I felt was some confirmation that we were headed in the right direction. Danny gets excited about things. He was excited, for sure, about missions, but he was also excited about what I had sent him in the email. He asked me to share it with the whole congregation that next Sunday morning.

So there I was, four months into my pregnancy with Bronner, standing up in front of that huge congregation giving a testimony about missions and about the work we have to do as Christians in this world, and I think it's just another hint as to why Bronner was given to me in the first place.

I still have that email, and I'm going to share it with you:

Dear Danny,

Hi. Just wanted to tell you about an amazing experience I had over the Christmas holidays that may give you encouragement that we have followed God's divine will in selecting New York as a missions partner and the good that comes from our Global Impact Celebration (GIC). Here goes.

I took Brandi, my stepdaughter, along with Rick's mom and sister, to New York, December 20–22. We had a wonderful time, no doubt, but the highlight of the trip for me came in the cab ride back to the airport to go home.

We were picked up at our hotel by a Muslim taxi driver named Mohammed. When I first saw him, I have to say I was a little nervous, and maybe a little afraid. My line of thinking was . . . Muslim, death, terror. But then, I remembered a missionary I had met and become friends with at our GIC, and how the people in Africa that she and her husband witness to are Muslim, and that gave me confidence. I thought, "If she can do it, I can, too."

It was God's intervention that put me up front with the cab driver. We began to talk, casually at first, then it became a full-blown spiritual discussion, and I gave him all that I had. I tried to explain to this man who Jesus is and why He came to earth. I told him that all men, including him, can seek and find salvation in Jesus Christ, and I have to say he seemed very interested and asked several questions—about who Moses was and about Adam and Eve. He gave me the ol' "Jesus was a prophet, someone took His place on the Cross," and I gave him the ol' *Case for Christ* response, "No, He couldn't be a prophet if He said He was the Son of God and wasn't. He either is who He says He is or He's lying. No prophet sent by God lies to us."

By the time we arrived at the airport, something had gotten through to him because he was thanking me for sharing with him and apologized if he had said anything to offend me! He said he was going to look into this some more and that he was going to get a Bible and read it.

You know, when I asked Mohammed how Muslims believe they earn salvation and eternal life, he didn't seem to know. He really had nothing to offer in defense of his religion, and that made a profound impression on me as a Christian. To me it was really a new revelation, and the experience deepened my own faith. God isn't stories in a book. What we know about Jesus Christ is true. Mohammed didn't have the answers . . . I did!

What I said to Mohammed is the only truth. It's the only viable explanation.

So this Christmas I came to realize how lucky—if you can call it that—how blessed, how miraculously favored I am. I know the truth. I am one of the very few people on earth who knows the whole story, and if I am this blessed and favored, shouldn't I be sharing this wonderful news more often? I mean . . . I hold the answers . . . we hold the answers . . . to life and death!

I'll tell you one last thing Mohammed said to me. He said, "You know, people in New York are not religious. If I am to hear this, I have to hear it from someone from Alabama or some place like that."

If New York is not religious, like he says, then we are the ones who are called to share this message with them, and I know I can't wait to go back to New York on a missions trip when the Lord calls me.

In fellowship,

Sherri

That email, I believe, is just another piece of the puzzle. Bronner was still in my womb at the time, but his life would prove to have a message attached. And he would make me dig deeper into these issues of life and death than anything else ever had.

There were a couple of other strange little twinges here and there such as the time I was at the zoo with Bronner and heard a whisper, something in the spirit, that made me stop and reflect on why I had this perfectly beautiful baby with me. It was one of those simply perfect days. The sun was shining. Bronner was shining. The zoo was shining. Everything was beautiful.

It was August 2007, and the older boys had started back to school. Brody was starting first grade that year, and would be in Mrs. Bandy's class. Brooks was going into second grade. He was two years older than Brody in age, but he had done a transitional class between kindergarten and first grade, which is a common thing for boys at Briarwood Christian School to do, so Brooks is only one year ahead of Brody by grade.

(Brody could have done the transitional class, too, but I think he was supposed to be with the teacher he was with during the worst thing that had ever happened to him as a child. That sweet teacher of Brody's reminded me of something after God took Bronner that January, when I couldn't see anything good in this world anymore. She said, "Try to look at it through the eyes of a first grader. Brody's fine. If he has his friends around him, he's happy. There's good left for Brody in this world, and you have be to here for him.")

We had had such a wonderful summer together that year, and Bronner, being used to having Brooks and Brody around all the time, was missing them. So I planned this special day for just Bronner and me, and, of course, it involved the zoo. Bronner loved the zoo. He would ask for it. He would say, "I go zoo." We went straight to the Birmingham Zoo after we dropped Brooks and Brody off at school, but it didn't open for another hour, so we went across the street to the botanical gardens. It was perfect because my "little runner" got to dash down those long paths and go exploring through the woods. I have some great pictures of him there in his little green Crocs and john-john suit. He was so cute. We had such a good time, him playing and me watching him investigate everything around him, picking up sticks and wielding them as a sword at an invisible foe. But the zoo awaited, so off we went. Bronner knew that place like the back of his hand, and he ran down those well-worn paths examining every animal as if it were his first time there. He climbed up on the fence to check out the giraffes more closely and watched an active otter swim for a long time. He was so curious. I could never put him in a stroller in places like that. His little adventurous spirit knew exactly where he wanted to go and exactly what he wanted to see, so I watched him as he rounded the corner over by the children's zoo. He kind of spun around like an airplane as happy as happy can be, and in that moment I felt a small pang of hurt run through my heart. It was weird and only lasted for a moment. As I looked at all the wonder and beauty and curiosity and fun and sheer life that was bound up in this very small child, I thought, "I wish someone else could be here to see this." He was just too wonderful to keep all to myself.

I've never forgotten that. It was a small thought but very real. It was a most beautiful day, Mommy and Bronner having a grand time together, but something was missing. Something wasn't right. Maybe it was an angel who whispered that thought into my mind. Maybe it was the Holy Spirit, but something, someone, said to my heart on that day that Bronner was meant to be shared.

And now, we are sharing him—sharing him with you, and sharing him with God.

There was another time something like that happened. There was a new *VeggieTales* movie released in theaters on January 11, 2008, and Bronner and I went to see it. It was deer hunting season in Alabama, and even though Brooks and Brody were only six and eight years old at the time, Rick was teaching them to hunt. I don't think they actually hunted. I think they just sat in the hunting stand with Rick, watching and learning what to look for. I thought it was great for the older boys to get to do manly things with their dad, and I didn't mind being left alone with sweet Bronner.

That hunting season provided me with lots of one-on-one memories of just Bronner and me, like the night we went to Johnny Rockets to eat together. I still remember the booth we sat in. Bronner kind of bounced around in his seat dancing to 50s music while he ate his chicken fingers and fries, and then he was ready to run. And he did, those little legs going as fast as they could down the sidewalk all the way from one end of The Summit Shopping Center to the other, stopping only for really interesting things like the toy soldiers in front of the Apple Store. He had on the "I Love Jesus" toboggan his Uncle Jamie had given him for Christmas and had just a little tuft of that red hair showing in the back, but his sweet face was gleaming with joy at just being outside. He loved being outside. I remember people commenting on his cuteness that night. One man said, "What a doll!" And he watched him take off, "Look at him a go!" I did, and I smiled at the man as I beamed from way down deep inside because Bronner was with me.

But this was another night, a more quiet night. We weren't at The Summit. We were walking into the Rave Theater at the Lee Branch Shopping Center near our house. It's a much smaller and less populated area. It was dark outside, and there was nobody else really around. I was carrying him in my arms and on my hip and had just gotten him out of his car seat in the parking lot when he pointed up into the night sky and asked, "What's that?"

I looked up to see what he might be talking about, but it was a clear night. All I could see were the moon and the stars. I knew that's not what he was talking about because Bronner knew what the moon and the stars were. We had talked about them many times before, and who hasn't read *Goodnight Moon* to their child over and over again? But I didn't see anything else. I looked back down at his face and saw that he was looking at me like he really wanted to know. But I couldn't answer that. I looked him in those searching eyes, and I said, "I don't know." Because I knew he was seeing something I couldn't see, even then. Now I look back and realize that that sweet baby may have been seeing something in that night's sky that was very, very bright and beautiful, that he, too, may have been given a glimmer of heaven. He had been mine.

THE COLDEST, DARKEST NIGHT

Psalm 127:3 says, "Behold, children are a heritage from the LORD, the fruit of the womb a reward." But this psalm also says, "Unless the LORD builds the house, those who build it labor in vain," and "Unless the LORD watches over a city, the watchman stays awake in vain" (v. 1).

I had a dream one night after Bronner had gone to heaven. In the dream, Bronner kept getting outside somehow, and I would find him out there, bring him back inside, and lock the doors. But he kept getting out anyway, and I was so frantic, in the dream, to keep him inside with me. The last time I went out to get him, I opened the basement door and saw him in front of me, sort of eye level, swimming through a wall of water that was before me. He didn't have on any clothes, and he looked just like he did when we used to give him a bath. We always thought he looked kind of like a Valentine's cupid because he had milky smooth skin, full red lips, and strawberry hair. He was so beautiful. And in the dream, he was still just as beautiful. He had a huge smile on his face, and his hair was kind of just flowing gently through the water. He looked happy, very, very happy.

"A man's heart plans his way, but the Lord directs his steps" (Proverbs 16:9 NKJV).

I got a call, soon after Bronner went to heaven, from a woman whose young son had also drowned . . . on the day Bronner was born. I knew that must be significant. I saved her message on my answering machine, and later, when I had the strength, I would call her back. Months passed before I finally did. The woman was also from Alabama. She told me her story and mentioned a book she wanted to send to me. I had called her on a weekday while my boys were in school. That Saturday night, or probably more in the waking moments of Sunday morning because I woke up thinking about it, was when I had the dream. I told Rick about it, but neither of us had time to process it before we had to get ready for church. The next day, Monday, I received the book in the mail that the woman who called had sent to me.

I became immersed in this century-old story of how a young mother fell ill while traveling and had to find refuge in the home of strangers. In the book, the sick woman prays for God's comfort, and is brought into heaven somehow. Maybe it was a dream, or a vision, I don't know, but what was amazing to me was the very first thing she portrays of heaven in the book is the River of Life. I knew that the timing of that gift to me was no accident. God gave me a dream, and the very next day, He gave me a tool to help me to understand what it meant. I realized my dream had been more than a dream. It had been a glimpse into Bronner's reality, the truth of his circumstance, a vision of rapture as he swam through the River of Life, just as was described on the pages before me. God has said,

Fear not, for I have redeemed you; I have called you by name, you are mine. When you pass through the waters, I will be with you; and through the rivers, they shall not overwhelm you; when you walk through fire you shall not

be burned, and the flame shall not consume you. For I am
the LORD your God, the Holy One of Israel, Your Savior.

—ISAIAH 43:1–3

God's provision is deep and wide, always giving us exactly what we need exactly when we need it.

"Oh, the depth of the riches and wisdom and knowledge of God! How unsearchable are his judgments and how inscrutable his ways!" (Romans 11:33).

The weekend it happened, Rick was out of town. He left Wednesday after work for a hunting trip and then on to a youth retreat where he would be speaking. It was our weekend to have Brandi and Blake, but they decided to wait to come over until the next weekend when their daddy would be home. (We never really stuck to schedules with them. They came and went as they pleased, pretty much.) That left me with Brooks, who was almost nine years old; Brody, six and a half; and Bronner, two and a half. I told Rick that I would be fine, to go, and to have a great weekend. When I talked to him on Thursday night, the biggest problem I had was the fact that I had attempted to make a scheduled dermatology appointment for Brooks to have a wart looked at. That meant I had to take all three boys with me, which was really not the norm for us. Bronner had been kept on a great schedule ever since he was born with very few exceptions, but he was older now. I thought he could handle missing his afternoon nap. Oh, but was I wrong. He was beside himself at that dermatologist's office, running through the lobby, behind the counter, and into their filing system. He was screaming by the time we got back to see the dermatologist, and I knew I had made a mistake. I should have cancelled that appointment immediately after realizing Rick would be gone that day, and I told him that.

It was one of the coldest Januarys we'd had in Alabama in a while that year. Snow was in the forecast for the weekend. It hadn't snowed in Alabama in years. I know this because Brody hadn't experienced snow locally since he was a very small baby, much to his chagrin, by the way. His two-year-old mother's day out class had had a unit on snow that must have fascinated him because he began to pray for snow every night. This went on during the winter months for years until Rick and I began to feel sorry for him. We decided to take him, along with Brooks and Bronner, who was around six months old at the time, to Gatlinburg when snow was in the forecast there. They had all been thrilled, but I had a bigger plan in mind. I wanted to take them to see some *real* snow. We planned a trip to visit Colorado with the Busseys, the family of Rick's cohost on *The Rick and Bubba Show*, during spring break that same year. Brandi went, but Blake did a trip to Hawaii with his school, so he wasn't with us. And Lindsey Harris came to help with Bronner. None of us had ever skied before, and I wanted to try it. I knew Bronner would have to be kept inside during his naptime, but I wanted him there to see the snow and to just be with us. He and Lindsey were able to go with Brandi and me on a walk around downtown one day. He was so cute all bundled up and strolling around in that Bugaboo stroller. And they went on a horse-drawn sleigh ride with us, that kind of thing. They

I was powerless in the face of death. I could do nothing. And when a person comes to that realization—that God alone can act, that God alone can change the situation—there's a reverence, a fear, a desperateness, a cry for help deep in the soul that He alone can answer. This realization is the very definition of humility, to see oneself in comparison to an Almighty and Ominipotent God.

just stayed in during the actual ski time. It was a great trip. And Brody could finally stop praying for snow, for goodness' sake! Interestingly, Breckenridge, Colorado, where we were, had record-breaking snow levels that year. I'm not surprised.

I had planned on going to my hometown of Lake Guntersville that weekend—the weekend it happened—to see my family and to stay with a friend who has a big house on the lake with plenty of room for me and my boys, but when I heard about the snow in the forecast, I thought maybe we should just stay home. I was talking with someone about it at my children's school, and he said, "Oh, you should go! The snow will be beautiful on the lake!" I thought it was a good point, so I packed up my three little boys and went. It was supposed to snow all over North Alabama, but it didn't. There was no snow on Lake Guntersville that weekend. It did, however, snow in Birmingham, where we live, but snow in our part of the country doesn't last long. It melts almost as quickly as it falls.

After spending the night on Friday night with my friend, Lesa, she and I took our kids to our parents' homes, just down the street from one another, and went for a long run along the lake. It was cold! But I was training for my "first" half marathon, and it was in the schedule to run several miles that weekend. It was the very first time my mother kept Bronner for me. He was two and a half, so I didn't mind staying out awhile. Lesa and I went to have coffee at a local coffee shop after our run, and we even dropped by a mountain gear type store. We were looking for winter running pants, which we both found and purchased. Then I went back to my mother's and spent the rest of the day there.

I remember picking Bronner up and taking him outside to see my dad's horses. And that afternoon, when he was getting kind of sleepy, I stood and held him in front of the fireplace and rocked him a little as I sang, "Baby mine, don't you cry. Baby mine, dry your eyes. Rest your head close to my heart, never to part, baby of mine." I knew the song from *Dumbo,* a very sad movie to me, but I loved the lyrics of that song. Bronner was my baby, and I never thought we would part.

I told my mom I had better get going with him before he got too fussy. She wanted me to stay another night, but I was supposed to teach Sunday School the next morning. So we loaded up in the big van and headed for home. When I say that the van was big, I mean *big.* It has a flat-screen TV in it, which is great for traveling with kids. I stopped at the local mom-and-pop gas station on my way out of Guntersville for some snacks for the boys. I popped in a *Bible Man* movie, one of Bronner's favorites, and we took off for the hour-and-a-half drive back to Birmingham. The boys also watched a *VeggieTales* movie on that drive. I remember which one. It was *LarryBoy and the Bad Apple.* I thought Bronner might fall asleep on the ride home, but he never did. By the time we got back into town, we could see a little bit of snow left on the tops of the houses and other things, which was very exciting for all of us. I would say, "Look, boys! Do you see the snow? Look! There's some!"

When we got home, it was already getting dark out, but we walked around in the yard for a little bit anyway. There were a few patches of snow here and there. I was holding Bronner and carrying him around, looking at it with the other boys. We picked up some and held it and tried to make a snowball out of it. I distinctly remember squatting down, still holding Bronner, and putting him on one knee, kind of in my lap, and him just looking at it, no reaction really, just looking at it. It was kind of funny!

I think I was probably more excited about the snow than any of the boys. As a mom, that's kind of how it is. I don't really get excited about seeing anything *unless* I'm showing it to them. If I happen to see a bunny or a deer, it doesn't really matter unless they're there to see it. I loved showing my boys new things when they were little. I'd take them to the zoo or some place like that, and say, "Do you see the giraffe? Where's the otter?" Showing the world to your kids is kind of the bomb! I loved it!

Then we went inside. It wasn't quite their bedtime yet, so I thought I'd just let them play for a while before I got them all ready for bed. Our basement has a movie room in it and a recreation room where the boys have their video games like their Nintendo Wii, which was what Brooks really liked at the time. So we all went down and got settled in. I put a Curious George movie on, locked the basement door to the outside, and made sure everybody had something to do before I went upstairs to take a quick bath. I hadn't had one since my cold run that morning, so I thought I'd get myself clean, then give Bronner a bath, and snuggle him up for a story and some love before bed.

Before I went up the stairs, I surveyed the area. Brody was lying on a beanbag type pillow in the floor of the movie room, watching the movie. Brooks was on one side of the couch in the recreation room playing his Wii, and Bronner was standing at the other end of the couch playing with some toys. They never even looked up as I walked by them.

I finished my bath, which is just my normal way of getting clean. I generally take baths instead of showers. I wasn't gone long. I had gotten into my pajamas and had gone upstairs to get Bronner's pj's, too. I was going to give him a bath in my bathtub, which was also kind of standard. I walked back downstairs to get Bronner for his bath. I expected to see him watching the movie with Brody in the movie room, the first room you see as you walk down the stairs. That was my thinking when I put the Curious George movie on. I thought it would pull Bronner in from the rec room, which is next to it and only separated from it by a hallway. There aren't any doors on either of the rooms. It's all just open. So I looked in the movie room where Brody was still watching that same Curious George video, and I said, "Where's Bronner?"

He looked at me and said, "I don't know."

Then I walked briskly to the next room, but he wasn't there, either. I said to Brooks, "Where's Bronner?"

His response was the same as Brody's had been, "I don't know." He was still holding his game controller and was still sitting on the side of the couch where I had last seen him, but Bronner wasn't there anymore.

Brody later told me that Bronner had, in fact, walked in and watched a little of the movie with him, but I guess it hadn't held his attention.

I went to the door, which only had a twist lock on it at the time. The lock was a temporary fix after the key to the deadbolt on that door had gotten broken off and stuck in the keyhole. Rick had gone by a local hardware store earlier that week with the intention of buying a new deadbolt, but they informed him that he would need to call a locksmith for that. He went ahead and bought a doorknob there with the intention of calling the locksmith when he got back from his trip. I didn't think anything about it. Why would a toddler want to go out in the dark and the cold when he was safe and warm inside with his brothers?

But as soon as I opened it, I saw him. He was floating in the water face down. I ran as fast as I could to get him. I grabbed him up and ran inside and laid him on the couch. I ripped the wet clothes off of him and tried to breathe into his lungs. They filled up with air but just collapsed right back down.

"The LORD God formed the man of dust from the ground and breathed into his nostrils the breath of life, and the man became a living creature" (Genesis 2:7).

I didn't have that kind of power. Only God, only God . . . I was powerless in the face of death. I could do nothing. And when a person comes to that realization—that God alone can act, that God alone can change the situation—there's a reverence, a fear, a desperateness, a cry for help deep in the soul that He alone can answer. This realization is the very definition of humility, to see oneself in comparison to an Almighty and Omnipotent God. This is also the point of perfect awe, to know, without any doubt, that He alone is God; He alone is mighty; He alone can help . . . or not.

"By the sweat of your face you shall eat bread, till you return to the ground, for out of it you were taken; for you are dust, and to dust you shall return" (Genesis 3:19).

My first real and concrete thought encapsulated everything I knew up to that point.

It's over.

My whole life—everything—was over. Not that I had given up yet. I thought he could be revived. I was hoping for resuscitation, but, even so, I knew that from that moment on nothing would ever be the same.

I screamed.

The other boys were both beside me, looking, as I was, incredulously upon their brother, not believing nor understanding what was happening. Frantically, I said to them, "Go get the neighbors!"

They knew the ones I meant, and they ran to get the doctor who lives next door. They used to swim in his family's pool before we got ours, and they loved their Jack Russell terrier, Gus, who, incidentally, likes to come over for a swim in our pool these days.

I grabbed Bronner up and went into Rick's office that was in the basement. I called 911 and told them that my baby had drowned. I hung up and ran upstairs with Bronner and put him in my bed and covered him up. I wanted to get his body temperature up. The doctor from next door walked into the room, and I said, "Do you know CPR?"

He nodded.

I gestured toward Bronner, and Dr. Feist began trying to revive him. I ran into my bathroom to get my anointing oil, and I noticed that the water was still running for Bronner's bath. I turned it off and hurried back to Bronner's side. The pajamas I had laid out for him were on my nightstand, waiting for a snuggly, clean baby boy to put on. I crawled up beside Bronner on the bed. I couldn't get to his head because Dr. Feist was there doing mouth-to-mouth resuscitation. So I poured some of the oil on the side of his tummy that I could get to, and I began to cry out to Jesus for the life of my child.

"Oh, God, please! Please, don't take him! Please give him back! Please, Jesus! Oh, God, please, please, please, don't take him. Please send him back. Oh God, please . . ."

I was begging.

I prayed so desperately for him.

Over and over I cried out to God.

An emergency responder entered the scene, grabbed Bronner, and took him to the emergency vehicle. The Feists stayed with Brooks and Brody. Everyone, even the emergency team, was in shock, I think, because the driver ran us into the ditch in front of my house. I have heard of people getting superhuman strength in times likes these, so I got out and tried to push it myself. I didn't have any superhuman strength that night. The vehicle didn't budge. While the crew was getting it unstuck, I ran inside, grabbed my cell phone, my phone/address book, and put on a robe. I was still wet from the pool.

Then a most vital, momentous, and crucial thing happened. A stirring way down deep in my soul said, *Not my will, but Thine, oh Lord, be done.*

I ran back out and jumped into the vehicle, and we started rolling down the road.

I could see the men working on Bronner from the front. They wouldn't let me back there with him. They put monitors and IVs of some sort on him. Of course, they were trying to jump-start his heart. I called Rick's cell phone number. He wouldn't answer. I tried again and again and again until he finally did answer.

He said he could feel his phone vibrating in his pocket as he was finishing up his fourth session of the evening. He was to do six that night. So as he wrapped up his speech to this fourth group with the words of John 16:33 and headed to the next auditorium where another gaggle of youth waited to hear him, he picked up.

"I have told you these things, so that in me you may have peace. In this world you will have trouble. But take heart! I have overcome the world" (John 16:33 NIV).

I told him what had happened, and his voice was just so calm.

He said, "What should I do?"

And I said emphatically, "Go out there and tell those people to pray! Bronner has drowned!"

"Where did it happen? In Guntersville or at home?"

"At home, in the pool," I said.

"We're on our way to Children's Hospital, and they're working on him right now. Pray that he doesn't have any brain damage . . . from the time without oxygen."

The thought of that perfectly beautiful little boy becoming something he wasn't was almost worse than thinking of him not coming back at all. But I wasn't thinking of that—yet. I wanted *all* of him. To have nothing of Bronner wasn't even a question at that point. I wanted him well and whole and himself.

Rick hung up about the time he was arriving backstage for what would have been his fifth 28-minute speech since 5:00. The evangelist putting on the event, Scott Dawson, is a great friend of ours. He said he looked up at Rick in that moment and saw something around him like a glow, a light, the Holy Spirit. Rick did what I asked him to do, and the whole youth conference began to pray for Bronner. Scott asked to go with Rick to meet me at the hospital in Birmingham, but Rick said, "Satan would want you to do just that, wouldn't he? No, you stay here and finish this. This is your work. Now, I have to go do mine."

I wanted as many prayer warriors as possible on this, so after I talked with Rick, I opened up my day planner to look for phone numbers of godly friends I knew He would listen to. That was before I had numbers saved in my phone, and I was always terrible at remembering them. The first number I came to was Linda's. "A" for Adler. She picked up and assured me that she and Michael would pray. (Michael Adler is the music minister at our church, and they were both good friends of ours at the time. They're even closer now, as you might imagine.)

"Can you call Danny? Make sure you call Danny. OK?"

She said she would.

I dialed Nana and Pop's house, Rick's parents, and Nana started screaming.

"No! *Please*, just pray!" I plead and hung up. I wanted the saints to intercede. I wanted God to intervene. I wanted the miracle. I wanted Bronner to live. I knew God had his life with Him already, but I also knew He could send it back.

Brandi answered the phone at her mom's house. I thought that Rick might have already called her, so I asked had she heard what happened. She said, "No." She hadn't. So I told her that Bronner had drowned, that we were on the way to the hospital with him, and to pray for him. She, like her dad, also seemed calm.

I didn't call any other family for fear of their reaction. I knew my mom would be hysterical. So I tried a few other friends. I didn't get many answers. It was Saturday night. I guess people were out. I did get Liz Whatley on her cell phone. She was a friend and also the principal at my kids' school. She said, "I have five praying women with me right now, and *we are on our knees.*" I knew she was telling me the truth.

As we arrived at the hospital and rushed down the hallway, there was such an urgency in the air and in our steps. I can see myself now as I look back on it, face forward, determined. I fell prostrate before the Lord upon entering the room where I trusted the doctors and nurses would do their part. I humbled myself, lying face down on the floor, in most earnest prayer. I looked up at the heart monitor at intervals checking for something, anything . . . but that straight line.

Nothing.

I saw them put the paddles to his chest as I went back down on my face. I looked up at it once more before kneeling over a chair to pray, but still there was nothing. Nothing. I remember a nurse holding out her hand for me to hold. She was down on the floor with me. I squeezed her hand so tightly. And I remember her face as she looked at me. It was filled with all the compassion and concern of that of a lifelong friend. It was an instantaneous exchange as I bowed my head and closed my eyes and asked God once again for the baby to come back.

All I wanted was my baby.

"God, please, don't do this."

Then a most vital, momentous, and crucial thing happened.

A stirring way down deep in my soul said, *Not my will, but Thine, oh Lord, be done.*

"Not *my* will, but Thine, oh Lord."

I didn't say that. I didn't pray that. I didn't want that. I wanted Bronner. But God, who lives in me through Christ and His Holy Spirit, prayed it for me. I felt the words rising up from within me almost as if I were hearing them, not deliberately thinking or saying them, but they were said anyway.

May God's will be done. *His*, not mine. That's how I knew that this was God's will. A strange calm came over me, a peace that didn't make sense.

I rose from the chair I had been kneeling over and stood to my feet. I took a few slow but deliberate steps toward Bronner. The doctor in charge came and stood beside me. He looked at me and said, "We're going to have to stop."

> But rise and stand upon your feet, for I have appeared to you for this purpose, to appoint you as a servant and witness to the things in which you have seen me and to those in which I will appear to you, delivering you from your people and from the Gentiles — to whom I am sending you to open their eyes, so that they may turn from darkness to light and from the power of Satan to God, that they may receive forgiveness of sins and a place among those who are sanctified by faith in me.
>
> —ACTS 26:16–18

And standing there, all alone except for the Spirit within me, I nodded my head and said, "OK."

Then they handed me my baby, and I held him and rocked him and sang to him, "Baby mine, don't you cry. Baby mine, dry your eyes. Rest your head close to my heart, never to part, baby of mine."

I sank back down on the floor with Bronner in my arms just holding him and rocking him. He was so beautiful. I never wanted to let him go.

And then Linda was there. She and Michael sat on the floor with me, and they cried with me and held my hand as I held my sweet baby for the last time for a very long time. Then I looked up and saw Danny standing there. I wanted him to have the answers. He was my pastor. I didn't say anything at first. I just looked at him searching his face for something. I guess I wanted him to tell me how this could be. Do things like this really happen? I couldn't believe it. I couldn't believe God would really take him away from me. I finally said, "It seems so final."

All Danny could muster in the moment was a sorrowful but matter of fact, "Yeah."

I guess he wanted me to believe that this really was happening, even if he couldn't believe it himself, for if the grief and shock and empathy didn't come out in his words, they were written all over his face.

Then someone came and took Bronner away from me. I don't know why. I think he may have been the coroner. Maybe he had to declare a time of death. I don't know. But he took him, and then they put him back on the table where they had been working on him and covered him up with sheets.

Someone asked me if I wanted to say good-bye. I went over to the table, or gurney, where he was lying, and kissed him and told him that I was sorry. "I'm sorry, baby. I'm so sorry this happened."

Then they asked me if I wanted to call Rick. I couldn't do it. I couldn't tell him. They said they could call him for me. They said that the chapel was filling up with friends and family. Did I want to see anyone?

I shook my head. I didn't want to face them. I didn't want to be the one to have to tell them that Bronner was gone. I didn't want to have to say the words, not yet.

Rick responded with, "You've really got a tough job, don't you?" And then Rick told her that he wanted to pray for her.

She came again asking, "Your friend, Leslie, wants to be here for you. Can she come back?"

At first I said no, but she insisted that Leslie told her that I would need her. Leslie's husband, Doug, came back with her. He's the landscape architect who had designed our pool. I looked at him and said something like, "I guess God didn't answer our prayer." I was referring to a prayer I had voiced with Rick and Doug and the man from the pool company doing the construction before we ever broke ground on the pool. I had asked that *no one* would ever drown in that pool and that God would use it to glorify Himself. Rick was the one who would later say to me that God had answered my prayer, just not in the way I had wanted Him to. He would use this for His glory. But I didn't see that yet. I was so dejected and confused and hurt by God that I couldn't see what He was doing. I wouldn't understand the why for some time yet.

I knew this was from Him from the very beginning. I believed that it was His will, but why? Why was it God's will? Why would He will this? I had never seen this side of God before. I had experienced His love and forgiveness, His blessing and even favor, but this? This was new. I didn't understand, and I was afraid.

We were all gathered into a little holding room, a small waiting room, and we waited there: me, Linda and Michael, Danny, Doug and Leslie, and Tarra Dawson, Scott's wife, who came just after we went to the new room. We waited together for Rick to arrive.

I asked so many questions that night.

"How do we know babies go to heaven?"

Danny said, "Because when David's baby died, he said, 'I shall go to him, but he will not return to me'" (2 Samuel 12:23).

But, of course babies go to heaven. Why would God send a precious baby to hell? He wouldn't. He doesn't. It's not in His character to condemn these innocent babies. And Bronner hadn't just ceased to exist. I knew he was somewhere. A life created *is*. A person can't be uncreated. Bronner's life is with the Author of Life in that beautiful land just beyond the horizon and just out of reach.

I wondered out loud if Rick would hate me. "Will he ever be able to love me again?" I asked the men in the room how they would feel if this had been one of their babies. "What if this had been your youngest son? What if this had been Brady or Ben? Could you forgive Linda or Leslie?"

"It's not about that!" Michael said. He seemed frustrated with my line of questioning. He knew, even if he couldn't verbalize it at the time, that God alone gives life and God alone can take it away. It wasn't my fault. It wasn't Rick's fault. As Danny would later say, in an email to Rick and to me, God was doing a work in our baby's dying that could not be done in any other way.

As we waited for Rick that night in the hospital, I remember my spirit was so uneasy and so troubled, and the handful of ministers and friends who were waiting with me seemed almost as distraught and unsettled as I was.

Meanwhile, Jordy Henson, a fiery friend who had fought spiritual battles with us before, drove Rick to the Tennessee airport where a small plane was being sent from Birmingham to pick him up. Jordy had accompanied his daughter to the youth conference that weekend in Pigeon Forge. As they drove, the prayers of 7,200 youth went up to heaven. The prayers were heard, no doubt, but the answer had been, "No."

"I called the hospital as we drove," Rick said, "but a chaplain picked up."

"Are you alone?"

That was all that needed to be said. Rick responded with, "You've really got a tough job, don't you?" And then Rick told her that he wanted to pray for her.

"Jordy was so upset, he pulled over for a time, and we prayed and grieved. We were both in shock. I could tell that he was angry," Rick said.

I've seen that anger before. It's a fighter's spirit that definitely has its place.

Rick called our families and told them. He said he asked them to try to be calm for my sake.

The man whose younger brother is buried next to Bronner now sent the plane for Rick. His mother had been with Liz Whatley in Highlands, North Carolina. Maybe that's how he knew. The pilot flying the plane was also a minister. Rick left Jordy there at their airport and boarded the plane alone. He and the pilot were the only two people on board that flight, but God was there. Rick said he looked out at the moon and the stars and said out loud, "What are You doing?" He said he just started talking to God like He was right there in the plane with him.

He was, Rick.

"The LORD is near to the brokenhearted" (Psalm 34:18).

"I prayed for You to protect my family, and I'm doing what I thought You wanted me to do. So what are You trying to teach me?"

God answered clearly if not audibly to Rick's spirit, *"I want the world to be perplexed. They think you love Me because I've blessed you. Your son is with Me, and I want your response to leave no doubt as to who I Am."*

Rick told me:

> I knew it was about the lost but also that it was about the church, and the word I kept hearing Him say was *apathy*.
>
> I knew what I had to do with the show and the platform He had given me, but I didn't know how to be what I needed to be for my wife and my kids. I kept thinking, *I've got to get to her.*
>
> I just wanted to get to you. I couldn't imagine you going through what you were going through without me. Every second I wasn't with you tore me apart.
>
> I kept saying, "I need to get to Sherri."
>
> I wanted to minimize the time.
>
> I told the four men who picked me up at the airport in Birmingham to take me to the hospital, Bubba, Kevin Kynerd, Speedy, and Mark Garnett, "Pray for me because I'm about to do the hardest thing I've ever had to do."
>
> When I stepped out, I could almost feel the presence of the Holy Spirit helping me to walk, helping me to stand, to walk that distance to where you were.
>
> I was about to walk into that hospital where you were and where our baby lay lifeless. It doesn't get any worse than that.

And then finally, there he was, walking through the door where I was waiting for him. His eyes went directly to me, and he walked over to where I was. I looked up into his eyes and cupped his face in my hands the way Bronner used to do. He sat down next to me and held me in his arms, and I felt safe with him.

A FATHER'S HEART

That's when I knew everything was going to be OK."

Michael was right. Everything changed when Rick showed up. He had already wrestled it out with God on that plane ride back from Tennessee, and he was ready. He was a hero that night, my hero, a knight in shining armor, tender and sweet to the damsel in distress, but also a warrior in the midst of a battlefield.

I wondered for a long time why God had Rick at a speaking event that night. The reason has only recently occurred to me: Rick empties himself of himself when he speaks, asking the Lord to fill him to overflowing with Himself, so that everything that comes from his lips is from the Spirit of God. He was already walking in the Spirit when he got my call. If he had not been, if he had still been hunting, who knows how he would have responded?

> *For those who live according to the flesh set their minds on the things of the flesh, but those who live according to the Spirit set their minds on the things of the Spirit. For to set the mind on the flesh is death, but to set the mind on the Spirit is life and peace.*
>
> —ROMANS 8:5–6

When a man is emptied of himself, only then can he be filled with the Spirit of God. The natural man is contrary to God. We all have inherited from that first man, Adam, a sin nature, but it didn't begin that way. We were created in the image of God with a spirit that desires relationship with our God. Only when a person sees his own spiritual sickness—the fallen state of his own being, the nastiness that lies just beneath the surface, crouched and ready to pounce upon him at every opportunity—only then does his soul cry out for relief. At that moment of realization, faith enters in, maybe as small as a mustard seed at first, and the Spirit of God comes to dwell within him and has communion with the man's own spirit that was indeed created for this very purpose.

This is only the very beginning of a sometimes long and arduous journey to the Celestial City where the faithful will look upon the face of God. There are tests along the way that aren't meant so much to check us out for worthiness, but they're rather meant to fit us for heaven. Faith is just a start in a walk with God. The earth is a place for testing, trying in the fire, refining, and we will sometimes fail or turn back and start over. But the process is meant to grow us from that smallest seed of all garden plants into an oak of righteousness planted by streams of living water at the hint of which new life springs.

When a person places their faith in Christ Jesus for the first time, that person receives the Holy Spirit as a helper and guide. If he or she is tempted to sin after that, the Holy Spirit convicts that person of the sin helping them to first recognize it, and second to resist. The resisting is up to the person. It becomes an act of the will, "Will I listen to the voice of God?" or "Will I listen to the voice of the serpent?"

Satan miscalculated this greatly.

That person may be so remarkably changed, even at first, from the former life, that he obeys God's Spirit within him. But he will undoubtedly come to a point when he chooses his own way once again. Then the Holy Spirit of God steps in to convict that person, showing him his sin over and over again until he repents of it. When he recognizes his own sin, asks for forgiveness from God through prayer, and turns away from the sin, there is growth in that person's Christian walk. This is one way we grow in faith and in the Spirit.

But this is not what I'm talking about on the night Bronner went to heaven. God had Rick at that youth conference, already on stage speaking, when I first tried to reach him. He had already emptied himself of his own will and asked God to use him as a vessel for His Spirit to speak through him. God ordained this so that the Spirit would immediately begin working. If Rick had still been on that hunting trip, things may have gone very differently. Rick may have taken a more natural approach and had a human response, but that wasn't to be. God made sure of that.

Rick's response wasn't human. It was spiritual from the very beginning. He seemed calm and at peace on the phone with me. He wasn't frantic or panicked, afraid or dismayed, but he was resolved and determined in everything he said and did. It was God working through him who prayed for that chaplain and who knew a man's true role as a husband, unlike Adam who watched his wife fall under the spell of Satan and, instead of protecting her, allowed her to lead him into temptation as well. Rick was no Adam on that night. He was more like Abraham who at once accepted God's will and obeyed. His every thought had been taken captive by God. There was a deep need in his soul to protect his wife, to guard me from the vultures who most assuredly would make an attempt to devour my soul and deliver me unto death.

And by vultures, I don't mean people. There was a battle in the heavenlies that night. And God, who is sovereign and glorious, omnipotent and mighty, a great God who goes to battle for, teaches, corrects, and reproves all at the same time, meant to be victorious—He sent a most gallant knight into service for Himself that night, strapping on that man the armor of Ephesians 6:10–17, yes, but also equipping His chosen servant with a Spirit that cannot lose.

"But you will receive power when the Holy Spirit has come upon you" (Acts 1:8).

"I equip you . . . that people may know, from the rising of the sun and from the west, that there is none besides me; I am the LORD, and there is no other" (Isaiah 45:5–6).

Willing vessel, witness, warrior . . .

And his foe?

The target of his attack was the leader of the opposing army himself, Satan.

The shining armor?

Jesus, for whom Satan is no match, not even close.

"And he said to them, 'I saw Satan fall like lightning from heaven'" (Luke 10:18).

"And night will be no more" (Revelation 22:5).

"I remember going over and kissing his cheek, 'cause I love that cheek, and I just said out loud, 'Satan, you *lose*! You *are not* going to win this!'"

Rick told me he didn't say it for the people in the room. "I said it for the 'great cloud of witnesses.' I knew there were angels and demons in the room watching and listening. I said it for them."

For we do not wrestle against flesh and blood, but against the rulers, against the authorities, against the cosmic powers over this present darkness, against the spiritual forces of evil in the heavenly places.

—Ephesians 6:12

Then Rick looked at his friends as he stood beside his son and told them, "Satan has *greatly* miscalculated this!"

"The God of peace will soon crush Satan under your feet" (Romans 16:20).

I stayed behind in the little holding room as the men went in with Rick to say good-bye to Bronner. I just couldn't go in there again, not while he was lying there on a table covered up in that white sheet. So I wasn't there when my husband grabbed the hands of the hospital staff still in that room and pleaded with them to get right with God right then and there.

Rick told me:

> I looked at the medical team with his little body lying there, and I said, "If there were ever a time someone could get a pass on being mad at God, right now would be one, but I'm not. Because of His mercy, I know my little boy is with Him awaiting me. Now the real question is, *What would happen to you if your body was on this table?* There is no better way for me to honor my little boy, and more so, my Savior, than by asking you this question, 'Are you a follower of Christ? What's going to happen to you?'" One person responded with "I'm Catholic," to which I countered, "I didn't ask you that. I asked, are you a follower of Christ?" And with that, the room went silent. I grabbed their hands and begged for God's mercy on the lives that might be lost and told them to cry out for Christ to save them if they didn't know Him. I found

out a few years later that the main doctor gave his life to Christ from that experience.

That doctor's parents came to hear Rick and me speak on marriage one night. They told us that their son was transformatively impacted by what had happened that night. He had watched, they said, as a mother cried out to God for the life of her son but stood at peace when she knew the answer was no. And he listened to a grieving father's challenge to lay down his life to Christ. And so he did.

"'You are my witnesses,' declares the LORD, 'and I am God'" (Isaiah 43:12).

Rick was indeed very bold that night, but he was hurting, too. He and I held each other in stunned silence as someone drove us home. We walked into that still house in the quiet of the night. Brandi had put Brooks and Brody to bed without telling them whether or not Bronner had pulled through, and then she had gone back home with her mother. But two of my brothers were still there, my mom and dad, Rick's mom and dad. Everyone had agreed before we got there that Rick and I should be the ones to tell the little ones, so the morning held for us that terrible job. Nobody said much. Nobody cried. In fact, I don't think I cried, really cried, for a long time. I remember looking around my kitchen trying to process what had just happened, what it all meant. I couldn't, though. I couldn't process it. I hopped up on my counter and sat there deflated just looking around. Bronner was gone. He wasn't there anymore. There was nothing to be said.

Then Brody's artwork on the refrigerator caught my eye, cotton ball sheep, his handprints in blue paint, construction paper cutouts of fish declaring, "I will make you fishers of men," and the familiar Shepherd's Psalm, Psalm 23, stilling my soul with its comforting song:

The LORD is my shepherd; I shall not want. He maketh me to lie down in green pastures: he leadeth me beside the still waters. He restoreth my soul: he leadeth me in the paths of righteousness for his name's sake. Yea, though I walk through the valley of the shadow of death, I will fear no evil; for thou art with me; thy rod and thy staff they comfort me. Thou preparest a table before me in the presence of mine enemies: thou anointest my head with oil; my cup runneth over. Surely goodness and mercy shall follow me all the days of my life: and I will dwell in the house of the LORD for ever.

—vv. 1–6 KJV

And just to the left of the refrigerator was a little painted board with a tiny silver cross in the top right-hand corner with this written underneath it, "Be still, and know that I am God" (Psalm 46:10). And in that murky, brownish paint, I thought I could make out a figure reaching down and lifting someone very small up and out of the deep. I can still see it in the paint today, Jesus lifting Bronner out of that water just as he was beginning to sink, just as he had with Peter so many years ago.

Rick thanked everyone for coming. Then he looked at me, not really knowing what to do next, so he asked me, "Do you think we should go to bed?"

I shrugged.

I have no idea what time it was when we finally laid down for the night, and I certainly don't remember falling asleep or how long it might have been that we slept. Maybe it was only from utter exhaustion that we could sleep at all; I don't know. But when we woke up Sunday morning, I had a clear message from God pressed upon my heart.

Rick is not your helper; you're his.

That's it. I sat up in bed, looked at Rick, and told him, "God just said to me, 'Rick is not your helper; you're his.'"

It was so odd. I didn't even try to process it then, but it's evident now that God wanted me to know that Rick was going to need me, too. This wasn't just Rick's battle. It was mine, too. I needed to get in there and help Rick, for that is what I was created to do.

> *Then the LORD God said, "It is not good that the man should be alone; I will make him a helper fit for him" . . . So the LORD God caused a deep sleep to fall upon the man, and while he slept took one of his ribs and closed up its place with flesh. And the rib that the LORD God had taken from the man he made into a woman and brought her to the man. Then the man said, "This at last is bone of my bones and flesh of my flesh; she shall be called Woman, because she was taken out of Man."*
>
> —GENESIS 2:18–23

Sometime later, God gave Rick a dream in which he was battling a demon. He was screaming Scripture at what looked like a woman dressed as a gypsy, and she was screaming back at him. He fought with this demon, he said, for what seemed like hours before he grew tired and had to sit down. But when he sat down, I stood up, and I started battling the demon in his place.

Rick and I have each other's back for sure. I will fight for him, and he will fight for me. And we will both be fighting for God, always. We stand armed and ready. We may have been wounded, deeply wounded, and we may grow weary from time to time because this world will wear on you. But we don't give up. We stand. We persevere. We endure. But first and foremost, we love. We love each other, and we love God. We're a team: me, God, Rick, and all of you who stand with us in defense of the faith, the Christian faith, the truth, the way, the life.

But Rick and God were going to have to carry me for a while yet. That morning was strange, surreal even. I had other children to think about. I got up and started frying bacon for breakfast. The teaching director from my Community Bible Study came early that morning. She was the first person to come that day. I don't remember what she said, just that I loved her like a mother and that her coming meant so much to me. The next person was her daughter, Stacy, a true sister. She didn't know what to say. Who would know what to say at a time like that? So she started to leave, too soon for me. I said, "Don't leave. Pray."

But she did leave. And Rick and I were left alone again. We went upstairs to the boys' rooms. With his sleepy eyes barely opened yet, Brooks asked, "Did Bronner make it?"

We had to shake our heads, "No." Then, I remember Brody's little head bowed down with one of his arms around me and one around Rick just nodding, accepting, trusting.

Then people began to arrive, lots of them. Many had heard the news from the pulpits of churches around the city. There was so much hustle and bustle going on in that house, women of God preparing way too much food that no one felt like eating. I sent the sweet women we knew from the children's school to watch over Brooks and Brody as I collapsed into a fetal position on the couch. My friends sat across from me asking what they could do. What could they do? There was nothing that could be done. Brandi sat at my

That baby's gettin' a "Well done." That little evangelist is whipping all of us right now by how many people he's bringing to Christ.

feet, and I handed her my Bible. I was too weak to read it, so I asked her to read Romans 8 to me. She did.

"Read it again."

She did.

"Again."

She did.

And it soothed my soul.

> *There is therefore now no condemnation for those who are in Christ Jesus. For the law of the Spirit of life has set you free in Christ Jesus from the law of sin and death.*
>
> —ROMANS 8:1–2

> *The Spirit himself bears witness with our spirit that we are children of God, and if children, then heirs — heirs of God and fellow heirs with Christ,* **provided *we suffer with him in order that we may also be glorified with him.***
>
> —ROMANS 8:16–17 (AUTHOR'S EMPHASIS)

> *And we know that for those who love God all things work together for good, for those who are called according to his purpose.*
>
> —ROMANS 8:28

> *Who is to condemn? Christ Jesus is the one who died — more than that, who was raised — who is at the right hand of God, who indeed is interceding for us.*
>
> —ROMANS 8:34

> *For I am sure that neither death nor life, nor angels nor rulers, nor things present nor things to come, nor powers,*

nor height nor depth, nor anything else in all creation,
will be able to separate us from the love of God in Christ
Jesus our Lord.

—ROMANS 8:38–39

I knew where to go because just that week—*that week*—we had studied Romans 8 in Community Bible Study. That was not a coincidence. God did that. He *would* work this together for good, but I was hurting. He was going to have to pick me up and nurse me back to health, and He would. He did. I am only just beginning to tell you what all God did. He held me in the palm of His hand and whispered to me the truth. Rick had championed me that night in the hospital, but God was going to bear the brunt of the work. Sometimes I felt like I was in a cocoon, like a force field surrounded me that nothing evil could penetrate, that I was being held in His righteous right hand and covered beneath the plumage of His wing.

God has taken me on a journey that has brought me to my knees, flat on my face, and flat on my back staring up into the sky ready to give up my spirit, and onto a plain of spirituality that plunges into the depths of God's heart and heralds His return. I used to think that I was walking through the valley of the shadow of death, but I wasn't, not then anyway. I was walking in the shadow of His wing. Nothing was

He suffered a gruesome, humiliating death because our sin is so nasty. And He died on that Cross for you and me, and this is the part some of you need to get, *when He didn't have to.* Some of you walk around like you had that coming. You didn't have that coming. You don't deserve that. You had hell coming, but He died for you anyway, and He suffered for you anyway, when He didn't have to.

dead, not really, no one I knew anyway. Not me, not Bronner. There was a death of naivety, of ignorance, I suppose, for I have learned more of God since January 19, 2008, than I had in all the years prior to that cold, winter's night.

My Bible became my constant companion. I held it and caressed it, even sleeping with it on my chest because that's where I found the answers. The "why" screamed from its pages. But I was thick of skull, and it would take a long time for me to understand what I really wanted to know.

Why?

But my warring husband seemed to get it from the start and took the battle into the pulpit that Tuesday with a sermon I am just beginning to comprehend five years after the fact.

Everyone stood amazed by what my husband, still operating under the Holy Spirit, was able to say on the Tuesday that we buried our beautiful son. I hope it can minister to you as well:

> You know, this opportunity that has been given to me today is an awesome opportunity. It's one that I think most of us would say, "I wish we were not given." But if you walk with the Lord the way our family has walked with the Lord for many, many years . . . see, and I don't say this pridefully. I'm just talking to all of you who are here. Some of you are my brothers and sisters in Christ, and your prayers and your support and your love have overwhelmed our family. But I will tell you this: I'm not surprised by it. I wasn't caught off guard by it because Scripture says that the world will know us by our love for each other, that it will be unique. It will be peculiar and it will overcome anything. And you have done that. You have showered us with love that is appreciated and

has helped us, but it has not surprised us. So thank you to everybody. There have been so many.

Another thing that a lot of people have said to me—and they've said it many times—they've said, "Are you sure that you want to get up and say something at this time?" And, again, I know a lot of you may not understand when I say that that is a very easy answer for us. And the answer is, "Of course, I do." Because, as I stand here before you today in this difficult time for our entire family, this is an opportunity that was given to me to leave here today knowing that I was obedient to my Father in heaven, to Bronner's Father in heaven, who is in the care of the only Father who loves him more than me. If you were to leave your children in someone's hands, and they said, "You're going. Who would you like to take care of your child until you get back?" Wouldn't you love it if they said, "I tell you what, I'll find somebody who loves your child more than you do." Well, see, that's our situation. Though we miss him and will miss him for years and years to come, according to how long God keeps us here, we know that he is in the care of a Father who loves him more than I do, the Father that he really belongs to.

It was funny because I was sitting here, and we were celebrating him. I was thinking about how he never got to come to "big church." And I know a lot of you who knew him know that he could not be in big church without you knowing he was in big church. And I realized that people are singing songs celebrating him today in "big church." I thought about Casting Crowns, again brothers and sisters in Christ, who immediately without question, said, "We want to be there." And I thought to myself, "You know, everybody loves a child," which is why Jesus loved the children and wishes we would be more like them. I realize if it was my turn to go on in, y'all are so busy you would probably have said, "We'd love to have been there, but we ain't coming for Rick." But I knew you would come for him. There's just something special about a child.

I remember when Sherri was coming up with the name Bronner. I remember thinking to myself, "That sounds like somebody's last name." She kept sticking with, "I want Bronner. I want Bronner." And I realize as I looked today on the handout, and I looked at this and all the things that have happened in his name, he was given a unique name so you wouldn't forget it. William Bronner Burgess will be remembered, hopefully, by you, forever because of the impact he will have for the kingdom of God, not the impact that he had for us that knew him as a child. I sit here today, and I look at my four other children, I've been trying to teach you, and as I stand here and do this, the second hardest thing I've ever done, I want to take this opportunity to challenge you in front of fellow believers that it is so much more important that you be warriors for the kingdom of God than anything else. I remember Sherri and me worrying about where you would go to school, worrying about what your vocation would be, worrying about what worldly things you would accomplish, and God convicted us so clearly. He said, "I will take care of that. You be about the business of teaching them to be warriors for My kingdom." So my prayer has changed. All I pray for is that you will have an impact for the kingdom of God. You will not be defined by anything you accomplish in this world. You will only be defined by what you do for Him. You are to be warriors for Him. You are to fight for Him, and you are to bring people to know Him so they will not perish. That is what your mother and I pray for you, and that's all that we're going to try to teach you to do.

Little did we know that as that process was going, God would take the baby and let him be the first warrior of the Burgess children—and what an impact that little fellow has already had. Those of you, I mean, I feel like I'm getting in late in the game. I mean there have been so many lives that have already been changed because of the appointment that God had with him. I had people, as I stood here last night, I had a person come up to me, and she said, "I shared the gospel of Jesus Christ for the very first time in the name of William Bronner Burgess." I had another man stop and say, "Listening to the story and listening to the challenge that Bubba and your wonderful brothers in Christ on the program gave in his name, when they said, 'If you want to help Rick and Sherri and their family, get your spiritual life in order and get on the Great Commission.'" And that person said, "Three people in my office prayed to receive Christ." And that's just the beginning.

A lot of you are sitting here today, well all of you, you are in one of these situations: you are a fellow believer—or you think you are, or you claim to be—or you're lost. And I'm here to tell you today that if God would have sat down with me 'cause I don't want you to look at me and think that there's anything special about me because there's not. I am a wretched sinner, unworthy of God's grace, who received it. God gave me a godly woman as a wife, and Sherri Burgess stepped up in my life when no one else would. And we took each other's hand on the day we were married, the holiest day in our lives, and we knew that God had a plan for us. And this godly wife and outstanding, godly mother will have a huge impact on the kingdom through what she's done as my helper and what she's done for these children and what she was doing as that baby's mama. And the impact is already being felt. So if you sit here today, the biggest injustice you can do our family, the biggest injustice you can do our Savior, the biggest injustice you can do for our baby, is to leave here unchanged, to continue to be apathetic, weak, ineffective believers of Christ.

It ought to break our hearts, more than the loss of this baby, that in the last survey, over 90 percent of believers have never shared the gospel one time, never. See, when I was standing in Tennessee with Scott Dawson, we were at that conference, and the most horrible news a father could ever receive came. And he looked at me because he loves me and he is one of my dear friends in Christ, and he said, "I don't know what to do." I'm paraphrasing 'cause it's hard to remember. I remember there was a time of confusion. "Do we continue this conference? Obviously we've got to get you home." And he said, "What do we do?" And he felt like, as any friend would, "I need to go with you." Well, thankfully, God had some of my other brothers set up there and here. And I said to him—because the minute that this happened, I knew what God wanted me to do. And I don't say that because of any pride in my flesh. I'm saying that because I walk with Him. I pray with Him. I talk to Him. And when I told Him I would be ready, and then He said, "Are you ready?" I didn't want to say, "Well, no. I'm caught off guard by this." 'Cause He wasn't wringing His hands about it, and you know what, I wasn't either. And I looked at Scott, and I said, "My son is in heaven, without question, because Scripture tells me where he is." God had a reason for allowing it. I don't think that God took our son. I think He allowed him to be taken at this time. The Bible says, "All of our days are numbered." Every one of us. And He allowed him to be taken so that He could be glorified and for no other reason, not to punish us, not to bring us heartache and pain. He did it so that the kingdom would be glorified, and I told Scott, I said, "My son's eternity is not in question, but 7,200 other people who are here at this conference, there are hundreds and thousands of them, their eternity hangs in the balance. So suck it up. Get out there and finish the fight because if we shut this conference down, Satan wins this situation, not Christ."

And, let me tell you something, Satan made a huge mistake attacking my family. Satan miscalculated this greatly. He should have never come after us. And when I say "family," I speak about this family, but I also speak about my family of believers because all of you have gone into action in a way that is making our Savior smile. If God asked me to give up a son so that some of you will live in eternity, it is well. But if God asked me to do this and you remain unchanged, well, that will break my heart. See, a lot of you are sitting here today and you're thinking, you know, "What are you going to do as a family? What do you do after something like this?" Sherri and I were talking about this. I looked at Sherri last night as we lay down for the evening, and I told her this—'cause this is really how my flesh feels—I told her this, I said, "I just want to go home. I don't want to be here anymore." I said, "I wish that all of us who love each other could just go to where he is. I don't want to be here anymore." It's not a great place. You know, things like this happen because we live in a fallen creation.

On the show, we deal with it all the time. People say, "Why would this happen? Why would God do this? I thought God loved us." Well, let me clear that up really quickly for all of you, OK? See, I was a sinner and you were a sinner bound for the lake of fire. Everybody in here deserves to go to hell, every one of us. And God looked at us, we had the gulf of sin between us, and He said, "They can't come to me; I've got to go to them." So He took on flesh of a baby, just like ours, born of a virgin, and He put on flesh, and He walked and He felt everything we feel. He was 100 percent man and 100 percent God. The reason I've already had a time of weeping—and there's more to come—is because He also wept, the human side of Him, when loved ones died. He also wept when He saw people He loved choosing Satan over Him. And He took on that flesh, and He suffered for you, and He suffered for me. He suffered a gruesome, humiliating death because our sin is so nasty. And He died on that Cross for you and me, and this is the part some of you need to get, when He didn't have to. Some of you walk around like you had that coming. You didn't have that coming. You don't deserve that. You had hell coming, but He died for you anyway, and He suffered for you anyway, when He didn't have to. And then He defeated death, and He walked out of the tomb on the third day to complete the job, ascended to heaven, which is what I'm going to get to next, and is preparing a place for you, when He didn't have to.

So, can y'all give me a break on, "I thought God loved us?" I think He's on record for how much He loves you and how much He loves me. So don't you ever take this situation and say, "I thought God loved Rick and Sherri and their family." He does love me. That's why He died for me. Anything else I get, I don't deserve because I didn't deserve that. How many of you are ready? How many of you are ready for God to take something that is so dear to you? How many of you are ready? How many of you just say that, but how many of you really believe it? How many of you really care if someone dies and goes to hell? How many of you sitting here today really have Christ as the center of everything you do, as the center of every decision you make?

In John 14, Jesus said, "Let not your hearts be troubled. Believe in God; believe also in me. In my Father's house are many rooms. If it were not so, would I have told you that I go to prepare a place for you? And if I go and prepare a place for you, I will come again and will take you to myself, that where I am you may be also. And you know the way to where I am going." Well, Thomas steps up, like a lot of us still keep doing, saying, "What are you talking about? We don't know how to get where you're going." Some of y'all don't know how to get where my son is. You don't have a clue. You say the right things, but you don't know. You can't know beyond a shadow of a doubt that if it were you who was taken, instead of my son, that you would know that you would spend eternity with Him, with Jesus Christ in heaven. If you can't answer that question, you've got problems.

And Thomas said, "How do we know?" And Jesus said, which sums it all up, "I am the way, and the truth, and the life. No one comes to the Father except through me." Some of you are here, and you believe in relative truth. Some are here, and you're buying some of the things that are being spun by the world, that there are many ways to heaven. Jesus Christ said otherwise. And if someone says, "Rick, you're a father who is hurting. You're just wanting to feel better, so you're saying that you know the way to heaven. And I tell you what, I don't know where you get off telling all us here. We came to support you, but we believe otherwise. You said Jesus is the only way to heaven." I didn't say it. Jesus did. It doesn't matter what I say. Jesus said it. So if you believe there's another way to heaven, take Jesus out because He took Himself out. He is the only way to heaven because He said it.

And, see, the thing about John 14, I had a pastor who was with me, who was there doing work and was working with the sheriff's department on Saturday night, and he said something to me that is so true because I felt God taking me in the same direction. He said, "You know, the great thing about John 14 is that it answers the question that is on our family's mind now." See, one of our loved ones has gone to be in heaven, and we want to be with him, but we're not. We don't decide when we go. Christ does. So what do we do in the meantime? Don't y'all all want to go home? But what do we do in the meantime?

Well Jesus said, "I'm going to prepare this place for you," and they're saying, "We want to go with you now." And Jesus said, "No, not now." And they said, "Well, what do we do in the meantime?" He said, "Well, in the meantime, you need to be about my business."

In John 14:15, He said, "If you love me, you will keep my commandments." God really changed me with that verse in the last four or five years of my walk with Him because I realize, and some of you are doing it here today, you are here today, at this service and your heart's being pulled. You're emotional and you are living a lifestyle, though you claim to be a believer, and you're living a lifestyle in conflict with our Savior. Do you know why you're living a life in conflict with our Savior and in conflict with His teachings? You know what Jesus said? "You're weak. You're pathetic, and every time you get a challenge you crumble because of a lack of love for Me." I didn't say it. It doesn't matter what I think. Christ said it.

He said, "Anyone who says they love Me will obey My teachings. Those who are against Me will disobey My teachings." It's really that simple, but it's powerful. I've learned that my disobedience is nothing but a lack of love for Christ. He said, "You don't love me enough to behave the way I told you to." And where we mess up, in the meantime, where we mess up—we mess up so much—is that we think we can do it. I remember talking with my older children, we were talking about the things that God's going to call you to do, the way God's told you to live. I acknowledged to them, and I acknowledge to all of us, I said, "Some of that's hard." And they said, "Dad, as a matter of fact, some of it's so hard, I don't know how we can do it." And I said, "Well, you can't. You've got to be totally submissive to Christ. Only He can do it."

Those of you who came up to me—and there have been so many of you—who said, "I don't know how you're standing here." And I said, "I'm not; He is." Some of you said, "How are you going to get up and speak?" I said, "I can't, but He can." Since I lost that little baby boy, it's really as simple as the simple, little, wonderful children's song. We've written some incredible songs. We've sung them today. You guys, Mark, y'all have written some powerful songs, but I'll bet you'd agree there ain't many of them more powerful than "Jesus loves me, this I know. I am weak, but He is strong. Yes, Jesus loves me." I am weak, but He is strong. I am pathetic, but He is wonderful, and He is speaking to you now because I can't. A father can't get up and do this. Only He can. Not an earthly father.

So I want to challenge you. I want to challenge you in the name of Jesus Christ and in honor of my son. See, when God had to give His Son, He did it, but you know what? He also got Him back. And I'm not strong enough. If God would have sat me down and said, "Rick, I love you. I need a son from you." I probably would have said, "I can't. I can't do that." And He knew that. That's why He allowed him to be taken without checking with me. But when it happened, I climbed on a plane because I have friends who love me, friends who didn't even know they'd be called into action, but they were, and they knew I needed to get home to my precious, wonderful, godly wife who was going through the most horrific thing a mama could ever go through. And a lot of you have been through it, and I appreciate you leaning on us and writing things to us. We're kind of a group who has something, now, in common that I know none of us wish we did. But I remember climbing on an airplane, and I had one hour. And I love that pilot, and I can't even think of his name, but he loves Jesus, too. And the plane I got on shouldn't have come back from Pigeon Forge in an hour. It should have taken longer than that, but he was letting that baby eat. I didn't know a prop would go 500 miles an hour. But I was getting ready to walk into the hospital, so I was on that airplane getting ready for that horrible moment, and I just sat there. Y'all have been there, fellow believers. You've been there when something tough's happening. And I just looked out that window, and I could see the moon and I could see the stars. And I said, "Hey, what are You doing, Father? Savior? What are we doing? What are You trying to teach me? This is a hard lesson." But, you know, by the time I got off that plane, I was ready. I was ready. I was almost instantly ready, but He really refined it in that hour. He said, "What I want from you is for you to go to the next level in spreading the gospel of the good news. Hundreds and thousands of people around the world are going to listen to you because you lost a little son, and that breaks everybody's heart. They're going to be watching you. They're going to be watching you. They're going to be watching your circle of fellow believers. The world will be looking going, 'How 'bout your God now?'" And He said, "I want them to be perplexed. I want them to look at you and your friends and say, 'How?' And you can say, 'We can't, but Christ can, and if you don't know Him, if you don't know Him, this world will devour you. And if you do know Him, be about His business, in the meantime, until He returns.'"

I want so much to go home to my baby and take my family with me, and we will. We'll get there, but if I left now, if Jesus Christ returned now, and I know a lot of you get tired and weary and you say, "I want to go home now." How many times do you run into somebody who says, "I wish Jesus would come back?" I don't. I don't. Not now. 'Cause, see, what God told me on that plane, He said, "If I come back now, if I bring you here to where your baby is now, people will perish; people will go to hell." So I'm going to be about His business more so than ever. More so than ever. More inspired than ever, which is where Satan made his mistake. But I cannot do it by myself. I want the death of our child to energize all believers to get about the business of preaching the gospel. Quit trying to be defined by what you do at work. Quit trying to be defined by what you accomplish in your hobbies. Quit trying to have your children be defined by how good they do in Little League or how good they do in the classroom or the lack thereof. Start being defined by the amount of people that you present the gospel to that God brings them to Him. Be defined as a father and a mother by how godly and powerful your children are as warriors for the kingdom of God. Because I gotta tell you something, there's one thing that our family feels right now: the stuff of this world don't mean nothing. It is fading away. It is fading away. I walked into my office where that little baby would always go in there and play, no matter how many times I told him not to. And he'd dump crayons out in the middle of the floor in my office.

I walked in there after he was gone, and they were lying in the floor. I just stepped on them and ground them in the carpet. Who cares? I leave the stain on that carpet. I couldn't care less about that stupid carpet. I tell you what I do care about, though. I care about standing in front of my Savior, looking around Him to William Bronner Burgess, and watching William Bronner Burgess hear from his Savior, "Well done. Well done."

Because I got news for you: that baby's gettin' a "well done." That little evangelist is whipping all of us right now by how many people he's bringing to Christ.

Don't let that happen. Don't let that happen. Jesus said to build up your treasures in heaven. We got a treasure already there. And you know what? I hope he is sitting there amongst a bunch of them because, honey, that's all that matters, is what we do from here, and what we do for our Savior. That's how we honor our son. That's how you could honor our son. If you're sitting here today and you don't know Jesus Christ as your Savior . . . the minute that I got this news, John 16:33 came to me, and, Scott, if you'll remember, that's the last thing I said at every session because I told them what the standard is and what Christ said we should do. I said, "But, you know, a lot of you are hurting, and what I've said is hard, and you're hurting." I said, "So let me tell you what else He said." He said, "In this world you will have trouble." See, I know we like to move on to the next part of this, which is so wonderful, but please don't miss what our Savior said. He speaks to trials and tribulations through Scripture much more than He does about good times. He said, "In this world you will have trouble." We, as the Burgess family, the Bodine family, and everybody who's connected to us, we're having trouble right now. But you know why we can make it? It's because He said, "But take heart because I have overcome the world." And that's exactly what I clung to when I got that terrible news. My Savior was standing right next to me. He had the Holy Spirit, the Comforter, right with me, and He was saying, "You're about to get some bad news, but take heart because I have overcome this, and I will be powerful where you are weak."

Do you know Him? Do you know Him? Do you know Jesus? Don't you want some of that? Don't you want that? Don't you wish that no matter what waited on you that you could look to the greatest Friend of all time, the greatest Comforter of all time? Those of you here who know Him and have access to that but you're living a pathetic, weak walk, I'm going to call for a lot of you to toughen up a little bit.

You're too easily defeated. You're too easily defeated! You get destroyed by nothing! Be strong. He gave His all for you. Give Him something! Stop this pathetic walk of, "I'm just barely going to get in, but I'm going to get in any-way." What a pathetic walk! Go in there expecting some treasures. Give Him all you've got 'cause He did. So that's my challenge to you. Don't let our Savior down. Don't let our baby be taken in vain. Make something happen.

As far as those of you who don't believe, I'm going to do what He asked me to do right now for you. If you don't know Jesus Christ as Your Savior, I want you to bow your head right now. Everybody bow. Those of you here who don't know Jesus Christ as your Savior, you came here because it was the kind, decent thing to do, and we appreciate that. But it is meaningless if you leave here lost.

I want you to pray this prayer with me:

Lord, I know that I'm a sinner. Oh Lord, I know I'm a sinner and need a Savior. And I acknowledge in my heart. Hear me now, acknowledge it in your heart. Words don't mean anything. It's your heart. *I acknowledge in my heart that I need a Savior, and that Savior is You, Jesus Christ. Lord, I want You to come into my heart, and I want You to forgive me of my sins. I want to repent from those sins and never walk that way again. I love You, not as much as You love me, but teach me to love You as much as You love me. Help me to walk as a new creation, to never be the same. Thank You, Jesus, for saving me, right now, in this moment. In His name I pray, amen.*

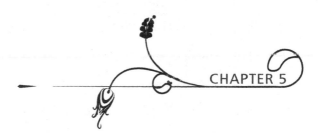

BUT I WANT YOU TO BE HOLY

The summer before all of this took place, I completed a study of the Book of Revelation and had been gripped by the knowledge that the present-day church is very similar to one presented in that book in not so great of terms. We are the Laodicean church. We are wretched, pitiable, poor, blind, and naked. We think we are rich and in need of nothing, but we are wrong. We are lukewarm, and Jesus, who gave the letter through the Apostle John to the church we are like, stands ready to spit us out of His mouth. But always, always, Jesus stands with an outstretched hand pleading with us to repent, to change, to be willing to walk through the fire and be cast into the furnace of affliction that we may shine brightly as refined gold. He asks us to open our eyes to see the truth set before us and to cover the shame of our nakedness with garments of white, pure and clean before Him. But the thing that hurt my spirit the most was the understanding that in my church, *my church*, Jesus could be standing outside knocking for admittance.

Oh, so much was going on in our church, so much good, but where was the spiritual fire? Where was this heat Jesus so desired of us? I determined right then and there to open the door to a knocking Savior that He might come into our sanctuary and live.

I almost forgot what we were there for, for just a moment, because this had become a sanctuary of praise for my soul and for my spirit that had become one with His Spirit, the Spirit of God.

Our family had always been fine in the balcony with what had become the equivalent of observing church. We moved to the floor near the front and became participants in worship for the first time. We came to worship God on Sunday mornings like never before. I began that summer, the summer of 2007, my last summer with Bronner, to raise my hands inside the sanctuary as we sang praise to the Lord. I was one of very few who did so at the time. And, slowly, hands started to rise all over that sanctuary. I don't want to take credit for this, but I do hope that my spiritual fervor was catching. Being closer to the front of the church also made it easier to get to the altar during prayertime. I fell to my knees at that altar many times and wept at my own lackluster walk. I had accepted God's blessings, but what had I given Him in return?

I was determined to give Him my all, to give Him true worship, acceptable worship, with reverence and awe, for our God is a consuming fire.

"Behold, I stand at the door and knock. If anyone hears my voice and opens the door, I will come in to him and eat with him, and he with me" (Revelation 3:20).

This is a verse often used as an appeal to unrepentant sinners to receive Jesus into their hearts as Savior and Lord. I say there is certainly no harm in that since God desires this from all people.

"The Lord . . . is patient toward you, not wishing that any should perish, but that all should reach repentance" (2 Peter 3:9).

But Jesus wasn't talking to lost sinners in Revelation 3:14–22. No, He was talking to a church, a very rich and prosperous church, one with lots of money to give and to do, one that had shut Him out of its services and didn't even know it. It was a startling revelation, a troubling one, but it could and would be remedied.

"Come in, my Jesus, come in, sit and sup with me and my friends. We welcome You, Lord." This was my prayer.

I was climbing the mountaintop for sure. I was singing with all of my might, with all of my soul, and I was drinking in the words of the message of God being given to me. Oh, how I loved Jesus!

It went on like this for a few months until that day I wasn't able to go to church on Sunday. I would enter that sanctuary on a Tuesday, instead, and I would behold a choir loft filled with every member who normally is seated there on a Sunday morning. I would see members of Casting Crowns ready to sing praise for what God can do even in the midst of a great storm. I would see my pastor handing over the microphone to my husband, who stood ready to challenge believers everywhere to make their salvation count for the kingdom of God. I saw thousands of people from every era of my life, childhood, college, family, friends, people from church, and from the kids' schools, everyone I knew and didn't know. The governor of our state was even there. And still vivid in my mind from the night before was that little blue coffin that I had helped pick out a day before that. It wasn't really there anymore, but I could still see it. I saw it there for a long time, in fact.

The visitation had been held on Monday evening and a graveside service that morning with a small group of family and friends. We had stood there for hours on Monday night as the line came by with precious people offering sympathy, empathy, and love, heartfelt

Life is not a pleasure cruise. It isn't about getting everything you want, nor is it about all the good you can receive *from* God. It's *about* God.

Everything in this life is preparing us for eternal life, and when we are no longer in love with the world as it is, when its seductions no longer satisfy, and when we are ready to move on to solid ground, then and only then are we free to really live as God is calling His children to live.

words of encouragement and truth. I remember someone asking me if I needed to sit down and me telling them that I could stand there all night if that's what it would take to honor my son. I love him so.

And, as our dear friend Michael Adler began leading worship that day and as his sweet wife, Linda, gave a testimony in song and as Mark Hall sang "Praise You in the Storm" and "Voice of Truth," I lifted my hand as high as I could reach, and I sang along and praised and worshiped God, who was and is and is to come, the Almighty. Holy is His name.

I almost forgot what we were there for, for just a moment, because this had become a sanctuary of praise for my soul and for my spirit that had become one with His Spirit, the Spirit of God. And when Rick began preaching that beautiful, convicting, glorious sermon to, for, and by His God, I had never, ever loved him more.

And I walked out of that sanctuary that day with a smile on my face.

"Naked I came from my mother's womb, and naked shall I return. The LORD gave, and the LORD has taken away; blessed be the name of the LORD" (Job 1:21).

I had praised the Lord with all of my might when my life was good and blessed of the Lord, and I had praised Him even more when it wasn't.

"Shall we receive good from God, and shall we not receive evil?" (Job 2:10).

These are surprising words from a man "blameless and upright, one who feared God and turned away from evil" (Job 1:1). Even Satan himself must have been surprised by Job's statement, for he had mocked God about His servant,

> *Does Job fear God for no reason? Have you not put a hedge around him and his house and all that he has, on every side? You have blessed the work of his hands, and his possessions have increased in the land. But stretch out your hand and touch all that he has, and he will curse you to your face.*
>
> —JOB 1:9–11

But Satan had been wrong about Job, and he had been wrong about Rick and about me. There were people who actually admitted to Rick that they had thought all this Jesus stuff he talked about on the radio was fake, but when he stood up that day and delivered that message at his own son's memorial service, they knew they had been wrong. It's easy to worship God when He gives you everything you want. We all know that. What's hard is worshiping Him when He doesn't, when He does something you never imagined He could, when He takes away something . . . unfathomable.

Job didn't lose one child. He lost ten, along with everything else: possessions, health, dignity, honor, friends, but never once during all of that testing did he let go of God. Yes, he wanted to know, "why?" We all want to know why—or I did. That was the thing I had to know.

Baffled, I looked up as unto His face and shook my head, wondering how He could take away my happiness, and said, "But we were so happy; we were so happy, God."

And He said, "But I want you to be holy."

I want you to understand, dear reader, that I was so broken at first, even though I could stand and smile and raise my hands in praise. I was so heartbroken. And the Lord, "The LORD is near to the brokenhearted and saves the crushed in spirit" (Psalm 34:18).

He was near to me, and I could hear Him. I could hear Him in my heart, soul, and spirit. I want you to understand that those words weren't something I made up in my mind. I wasn't talking to myself. I was imploring God. I was crying out in desperation, and He answered me. He answered.

"My sheep hear my voice" (John 10:27).

Maybe it was because I was truly like a sheep for the first time, completely dependent upon my Shepherd, beseeching, searching, seeking, knowing for certain that I couldn't live through this without Him. I didn't want anything from God. I wanted God. I was afraid. I didn't know the world could be so bad. I didn't know. And I needed my Father. Not only did He uphold me, He answered me.

When Elijah was despairing of life, God told him to go out and stand on the mount before Him.

> *And a great and strong wind tore the mountains and broke in pieces the rocks before the LORD, but the LORD was not in the wind. And after the wind an earthquake, but the LORD was not in the earthquake. And after the earthquake a fire, but the LORD was not in the fire. And after the fire the sound of a low whisper.*
>
> —1 KINGS 19:11–12

When this groaning creation rages against us and breaks apart every good thing we thought it held for us and we reach out for something more, something more than this life and this time, then . . . then we are ready to listen and hear.

I said, "But we were so happy; we were so happy, God."

And He said, "But I want you to be holy." As clear and as concise as that.

God was teaching me by His own Spirit what life was really about and what it was not about. He made it very clear that this life isn't about happiness or the pursuit

I have thought about what life would be like if this never had happened, how happy we would still be, but then I realized that our happiness would help no one but ourselves.

thereof. Life is not a pleasure cruise. It isn't about getting everything you want, nor is it about all the good you can receive *from* God. It's *about* God. We've heard it said so many times it's almost cliché, "Don't seek His hand; seek His face." But we do. There are entire ministries set aside to teach people how to get what they want from God. But God does not want this. God wants you and me to seek Him, to know Him, to love *Him*. He desires a relationship with us, and He wants us to desire a relationship with Him above all else.

When Jesus said, "I came that they may have life and have it abundantly" (John 10:10) or "to the full" as the New International Version puts it, He's talking about eternity. Some of us need to look up what the word *abundance* means. He's talking about quantity not quality for the here and now. Life abundant is life everlasting. Jesus came to give us eternal life, not "the good life." The here and now holds trouble for the Christian. That's what Jesus said. He sent His disciples out with nothing but the clothes on their backs. He never promised them that in this life they would have a lake house and a beach house and a Maserati ready to go. He told them that if the world hated Him, it was going to hate them also.

We are only sojourners on this earth. The heroes of faith from Hebrews 11—Abel, Enoch, Noah, Abraham, Sarah, Joseph, Moses— all died in faith:

> *Not having received the things promised, but having seen them and greeted them from afar, and having acknowledged that they were strangers and exiles on the earth. For people who speak thus make it clear that they are seeking a homeland. If they had been thinking of that land from which they had gone out, they would have had opportunity to return. But as it is, they desire a better country, that is, a heavenly one. Therefore God is not ashamed to be called their God, for he has prepared for them a city.*
>
> —HEBREWS 11:13–16

There is something greater, something better, something more wonderful out there that we can't see right now, a city with gates and foundations, a real city that will one day come down out of heaven from God, and the Bible says to behold it. Behold it. Hold it in our hearts. Long for it. Set your mind on it as Colossians 3:1–2 tells us. It's coming. He's coming. And I say, "Come, Lord Jesus; come quickly."

> *Behold, the dwelling place of God is with man. He will dwell with them, and they will be his people, and God himself will be with them as their God. He will wipe away every tear from their eyes, and death shall be no more, neither shall there be mourning, nor crying, nor pain anymore, for the former things have passed away.*
>
> —REVELATION 21:3–4

And he who was seated on the throne said, "Behold, I am making all things new."

—REVELATION 21:5

Can you imagine an earth made new, no longer fallen or cursed, where cancer is nonexistent, where the separation of death and sin are not allowed, where war is not heard of, and where there is no such thing as hunger or poverty? Can you imagine an earth as God intended it to be from the beginning, and maybe even better because all those who live there will have been tested and tried and humbled under the mighty hand of God and been found faithful and true sons of God who will not rise up against Him like Lucifer had?

I believe that may be the reason God allowed the fall of man in the first place. If an "anointed guardian cherub" (Ezekiel 28:14), who was endowed with wisdom and beauty and given every good thing, could fall so far as to be called *Satan, the adversary, devil, the accuser, the enemy of God*, wouldn't we fall, too? Of course we would! We did. We fell, just like Lucifer fell, but some of us God would call out from this fallen creation to become His true sons and daughters, unchained from this world and its power to entice, who choose the good portion, the best portion, the Bread of Life and Living Water, the Lord.

"*You shall be holy to me, for I the Lord am holy and have separated you from the peoples, that you should be mine*" (Leviticus 20:26).

The first time we see the word *holy* in the Bible is in Genesis 2:3, as God is talking of a day that would be different from all the other days.

God didn't ask me before he took my child from me, but when He did, I submitted to His will. I don't like it, but I understand it. I know that it's not forever. And it's forever that I'm in this for.

"So God blessed the seventh day and made it holy, because on it God rested from all his work that he had done in creation." So here we learn that to be holy is to be set apart, different. We're not supposed to be like everybody else. We are called to be different. We are called to be holy.

Then in Leviticus 20:7–8 we read, "Consecrate yourselves, therefore, and be holy, for I am the LORD your God. Keep my statutes and do them; I am the LORD who sanctifies you." God was now beginning to teach the Israelites His decrees and laws. And every time He would tell them to be holy like Him, He would follow it up with commandments, setting before them His standard of right and wrong, who He is, and what He expected of them. So we can now see that to be holy is to be set apart from the world, living above its definition of right and wrong, and to be kept within God's requirements according to His.

> As obedient children, do not be conformed to the passions of your former ignorance, but as he who called you is holy, you also be holy in all your conduct, since it is written, "You shall be holy, for I am holy." And if you call on him as Father who judges impartially according to each one's deeds, conduct yourselves with fear throughout the time of your exile, knowing that you were ransomed from the futile ways inherited from your forefathers, not with perishable things such as silver or gold, but with the precious blood of Christ, like that of a lamb without blemish or spot.
>
> —1 PETER 1:14–19

God wants His children to be different from the world because the prince of this world in this age is Satan, who is out to kill, steal, and destroy that which does not belong to him—us, for we are God's workmanship. We are His creation. The devil prowls around going in and out of the earth looking for someone to devour. He tried to devour me and my family, but God knew this would bring us even closer to the throne room of God.

That was His purpose in allowing it in the first place. Satan meant it for harm, yes, but God meant it for good.

God may have begun a revival in my spirit the summer before, but when He brought my baby into heaven with Him, my eyes were opened to the things that are above, things that cannot be shaken or removed or burned up by fire, to what thieves can't steal, moths eat, or rust destroy. And when, with such anointing salve, one's eyes have been so opened, apathy is utterly destroyed. God took the love of the world out of me and in so doing, He showed me what really matters. Everything in this life is preparing us for eternal life, and when we are no longer in love with the world as it is, when its seductions no longer satisfy, and when we are ready to move on to solid ground, then and only then are we free to really live as God is calling His children to live, as exiles and sojourners, storing up treasures for our real home, walking as children of light, and as a fragrant and pleasing aroma to the Lord, "a living sacrifice, holy and acceptable to God" (Romans 12:1).

"For we are his workmanship, created in Christ Jesus for good works, which God prepared beforehand, that we should walk in them" (Ephesians 2:10).

For Rick and me, our wedding day, February 10, 1996, had been the beginning of a beautiful work by the Potter's own hand. He took two lumps of clay and began sculpting them together into something very fine. He painted the piece with vibrant color and added precious gemstones. Anyone could see that it was a wonderfully happy and brilliant piece of work. But when God put what He had molded into the fire, He held it there until the colors

My little baby boy brought me that message from God, to live my life in the pursuit of holiness, not happiness, and in that pursuit not only would my weary soul find rest it would find peace.

faded and the gemstones fell away. All that was left was a plain, humble pot filled with tears and marked with sorrow. What had come out of that kiln, the fired work, was now something God could use. It's the firing process that gives sculpted clay its strength. Without it, the clay is useless. The fire sets the shape forever and makes it the pottery that it was designed to be all along. I have thought about what life would be like if this never had happened, how happy we would still be, but then I realized that our happiness would help no one but ourselves. God meant for us to be used, to bring others true joy, not just happiness, and in so doing we would find strength to stand and peace that transcends all understanding. In time, we would run again and not grow weary knowing that soon, and very soon, we would soar once more. Rick and I were always meant to be more like border collies, bred for work, than some of the more genteel breeds meant mainly to be stroked and petted. I don't want to be petted. I want to be used. I want to be a loyal companion for the Lord allowing Him to train me for the work of His pastures and following Him wherever He leads.

I loved God before and served Him the best I knew how, but God was going to take me far deeper with Him than my happy and blessed life ever could. God wasn't so interested in my immediate happiness as in my holiness and my joy forever. See, happiness and joy aren't the same thing. Joy comes from the Lord, in knowing Him and having a part with Him. Happiness comes and goes as quickly as the drive-through attendant can get your order wrong. You get home with a bag full of the wrong order, and your happiness is gone. See, because happiness is an emotion, a feeling, based on cir-cumstances, but the Bible teaches that a man's feelings are as flimsy as the wind. We are not to base our lives on feelings, but we are to base our lives on the Word of God.

And God's Word tells us to be holy over and over and over again. "Be holy, for the Lord your God is holy." Holiness is a defining char-acteristic of God, and it should be a defining characteristic of His people. I believe that holiness comes to the human heart through humility. In submitting to God's authority and sovereignty, we become servants and citizens of His kingdom. Through obedience, we become His children and heirs. In time, through faithfulness and quiet endurance that daily brings us to the feet of Jesus, we will find that we have been made a friend. Today as I sit writing, I know that Jesus is my best friend, who knows me by name, who called me long ago to Himself, and who has taught me to wear the white garments of Revelation 3:18 that are the holiness God requires of His people.

I'm spending a lot of time on this subject not only because it's the central truth God Himself spoke to me upon questioning Him but also because the Bible tells us in Hebrews 12:14 that without holiness, no one will see the Lord. That is a profound statement. "Strive for . . . the holiness without which no one will see the Lord." I find that all the discipline in the world is worth that. I want to see the Lord. I do not ever want to be cast out of His presence because I know that without Him there is nothing, no life, no peace, no joy, no love, nothing. I want God and all His holiness I can clothe myself in. I want to be taught of the Lord, no matter what that means for me. I trust that His plans for me are better than any I could dream up for myself. I don't always like His methods, but I can't argue the

> You and I were the joy set before Christ to make Him want to endure the Cross.

results. If I wasn't willing to give up my worldly pursuits for godly ones, if I continued "on the earth in luxury and in self-indulgence" (James 5:5), if I weren't willing to cast aside all things for the sake of Christ, then God would do it for me.

What wouldn't we do for the Lord? People are being asked even now to give up their very lives for God, and they're saying, "Yes." God didn't ask me before he took my child from me, but when He did, I submitted to His will. I don't like it, but I understand it. I know that it's not forever. And it's forever that I'm in this for. I'm in it for good. No going back. For Jesus said:

> *Whoever loves father or mother more than me is not worthy of me, and whoever loves son or daughter more than me is not worthy of me. And whoever does not take his cross and follow me is not worthy of me. Whoever finds his life will lose it, and whoever loses his life for my sake will find it.*
>
> —MATTHEW 10:37–39

I have learned that I can't live my life for myself anymore, for any worldly pleasure or gain. My treasure is in heaven, and I hope that I will continue to store up treasure there, that I will shine light in dark places, and that I will always remember to live my life as a living sacrifice to God, holy and acceptable.

My little baby boy brought me that message from God, to live my life in the pursuit of holiness, not happiness, and in that pursuit not only would my weary soul find rest, it would find peace. And in the midst of that peace, I would find hope, and hope wouldn't disappoint because in that hoping, I would find my joy in knowing that the best is yet to come. This knowledge gives me the strength I need to continue this long passage, to continue to fight, to grow, to learn, and to allow myself to be used for the glory of the kingdom of God.

If then you have been raised with Christ, seek the things that are above, where Christ is, seated at the right hand of God. Set your minds on things that are above, not on things that are on earth. For you have died, and your life is hidden with Christ in God. When Christ who is your life appears, then you also will appear with him in glory. Put to death therefore what is earthly in you: sexual immorality, impurity, passion, evil desire, and covetousness, which is idolatry. On account of these the wrath of God is coming. In these you too once walked, when you were living in them. But now you must put them all away: anger, wrath, malice, slander, and obscene talk from your mouth. Do not lie to one another, seeing that you have put off the old self with its practices and have put on the new self, which is being renewed in knowledge after the image of its creator. Here there is not Greek and Jew, circumcised and uncircumcised, barbarian, Scythian, slave, free; but Christ is all, and in all. Put on then, as God's chosen ones, holy and beloved, compassionate hearts, kindness, humility, meekness, and patience, bearing with one another and, if one has a complaint against another, forgiving each other; as the Lord has forgiven you, so you also must forgive. And above all these put on love, which binds everything together in perfect harmony. And let the peace of Christ rule in your hearts, to which indeed you were called in one body. And be thankful. Let the word of Christ dwell in you richly, teaching and admonishing one another in all wisdom, singing psalms and hymns and spiritual songs, with thankfulness in your hearts to God. And whatever you do, in word or deed, do everything

in the name of the Lord Jesus, giving thanks to God the
Father through Him.

—Colossians 3:1–17

And that is what God was talking about when He said, "But I want you to be holy."

He wasn't giving me a new command, just clearing up why He had allowed my happiness to be taken away. And let me be clear, I'm happy, I guess. But I'm not happy in the way that I was. I will never be happy in that way until I'm holding my baby in my arms again. That happiness is gone for now. That was a carefree, light, sweet happiness framed in innocence and ignorance. It is the difference between the Garden of Eden before Adam and Eve were cast out of it and then afterward. Adam and his wife ate from the tree of the knowledge of good and evil, and so have I. I understand what is good and what is evil, but that knowledge has come, as theirs did, at great cost.

> *Let us also lay aside every weight, and sin which clings*
> *so closely, and let us run with endurance the race that is*
> *set before us, looking to Jesus, the founder and perfecter of*
> *our faith, who for the joy that was set before him endured*
> *the cross, despising the shame, and is seated at the right*
> *hand of the throne of God.*
>
> —Hebrews 12:1–2

Jesus endured the Cross, the Bible tells us, for the joy set before Him, joy in knowing that He wasn't going to be the only one to die and then rise again. He would be the firstborn out of the grave of many brothers, and through Christ's sufferings, by His wounds, we would be healed. He saw before Him multitudes rising from the dead from every tongue, tribe, and nation, clothed in fine linen and made pure and perfect by His blood. He saw it all before Him, so he went to the Cross to fulfill the purpose for which He came.

Preparing Himself for the Cross, Jesus said, "Now is my soul troubled. And what shall I say? 'Father, save me from this hour'? But for this purpose I have come to this hour. Father, glorify your name" (John 12:27–28).

Jesus is our standard. We can't measure ourselves by anyone else because "all have sinned and fall short of the glory of God" (Romans 3:23). All but Jesus. He's the one we should imitate.

When our time of sorrow comes, and it will, we, like Jesus, should say:

> Father, glorify Your name. For this purpose You have given me life. Let this cup pass from me, yes, but . . . not my will, but Thine, O Lord, be done. I will stand upon the rock of my salvation, and I will proclaim Your greatness, Your power, Your comfort, Your mercy, Your goodness, and even Your joy forever. I will praise the name of Jesus. I will not turn to the left or to the right, but I will fix my gaze upon You, Father, and I will accept Your will.

You and I were the joy set before Christ to make Him want to endure the Cross. He saw us—His bride, the church, "bright and pure" (Revelation 19:8), and made ready for the marriage supper of the Lamb, His marriage. His bride would be ready to live with Him forever because of the suffering He would endure for her, and He asks His bride to do the same for Him, to see the joy set before us so we will be able to endure our own crosses now, to endure suffering and trial and persecution and tests of faith knowing that all of it is "preparing for us an eternal weight of glory beyond all comparison" (2 Corinthians 4:17). We are to endure now for the joy that is to come later, for the hallelujahs that are to come, and that joy is with us even now because of that expectation.

Yes, great joy has been set before me. Not only have I been given eternal life, which in and of itself is reason to rejoice. Thy grace is sufficient for me, but You, oh God, have promised so much more. You have not only redeemed my soul from the fires of hell, You've promised a new heaven and a new earth where sin and death are no more. You've promised that the holy city, new Jerusalem, will come down out of heaven and that you, oh God, will dwell here with us on earth.

Death and Hades will be thrown into the lake of fire, along with all the wicked and all those who have rebelled against God through unbelief, and all the powers of evil will be gone. No more will disease or sickness come upon anyone. The thorns and the thistles will be gone, and the animals . . . Listen to what Isaiah 11:6 says about the animals: "The wolf shall dwell with the lamb, and the leopard shall lie down with the young goat, and the calf and the lion and the fattened calf together; and a little child shall lead them."

Maybe that child will be Bronner.

And so we press on, knowing that the Lord is our refuge and high tower in our time of need. We run to Him, and He gives us comfort. And then He gives us strength, strength to endure and peace that transcends all understanding. I am at peace because I know in whom I have believed. I know God, and I know that the travail of losing a son and the glory God has received through it may be my life's greatest purpose.

"Now is my soul troubled. And what shall I say? 'Father, save me from this hour'? But for this purpose I have come to this hour. Father, glorify your name" (John 12:27–28).

CHILDREN OF A BROKENHEARTED PARENT

It was the animals that helped the almost nine-year-old Brooks to see that something wasn't right with the world but that God would some day make it right.

After Bronner's memorial service, I knew I didn't want to be at home for a while, so we headed to Jemison to stay in our little farmhouse there. We had only purchased it two and a half months before, which is absolutely providential because we weren't looking for a farm. God just seemed to give it to us. It wasn't even furnished yet, but sometime between Sunday and Tuesday, I called a friend who is a decorator and asked her to call another friend who owns a bedding shop to see if they wouldn't mind getting some mattresses and some bedding down there for us to sleep on. When we walked in that Tuesday night, everything was perfect. The two of them had not only brought what I had asked for, but they had completely furnished that farmhouse. And it was lovely, a beautiful gift on such a horrible day. They had thought of everything, too: dishes, towels . . . There was even food in the pantry. The wrought iron bed they had brought for Rick and me to sleep on had pretty baby blue linens, and the boys' new bunk bed looked as if it could have been in a cabin in the woods with its rustic fishing-themed bedding. There was even a small daybed for Brandi. It was perfect, just exactly what we needed, a cozy, little place to huddle together in as we weathered the storm as a family.

This was the desert place God took me to in order to speak tenderly to me. One night I was reading to the boys before bed from a little booklet called *Scripture Confessions for Kids* and came to this: "No one can take my joy from me, for Jesus is my joy and His joy makes me strong. (John 16:22; Nehemiah 8:10)."

After prayers and kisses, I went to the kitchen and ate a piece of chocolate. It was the first time I had done anything for myself since Bronner had been gone. I had kind of been going through the motions of life, trying to stay alive and taking care of my children, but when I read that Scripture truth that night, it registered with me. My joy wasn't gone. Jesus was with me now more than ever. Maybe I had thought Bronner was my joy, but God wanted me to know that I had been wrong. In that little farmhouse, God fed me the chicken soup of truth and began to nurse me back to life. I went outside one morning and found flowers blooming . . . in January! Everything else was so bleak and colorless, everywhere but on that one camellia bush and on my kitchen table. I saw those bright blooms as a kindness from God showing me that there is life yet to be lived.

Two of the biggest motivators for that life were the little boys God left for me to raise. Brandi and Blake were practically grown by that time, but Brooks and Brody were still very young. And they were all hurting. We all were. Brandi probably had the best reaction of all the kids, or at least the most immediately beneficial: maturation. She said she became a woman on January 19, 2008, and she did. As a teen, her life had been filled with accomplishments, one lead role right after the next. She was even on a local magazine cover as one of the top 20 high school seniors who would "change the world." I don't doubt that she will. But something changed in her for the good on that day. She came out of herself, so to speak, and jumped into her family like never before. She wanted to be with us at our farm, even if that meant driving herself to school every morning all the way to the Alabama School of Fine Arts in downtown Birmingham. She became the fun in our family, so silly, kooky, and youthful, just as I aged 20 years in a night. We needed her, and she came through.

Blake had the opposite reaction. He did not want to be with us. He had to work it all out on his own. He kept hearing everyone talk about all the good that had come about because of his perceived loss, and he didn't like it. "What about me?" he wanted to know.

I can't tell you how many people came to know the Lord for the first time through what happened to our family, but I do know it was many. At the memorial service alone, there were more than 200 decisions for Christ. We know this because the Scott Dawson Evangelistic Association provided decision cards in anticipation of Rick's invitation. But, even so, this was no ordinary earthly death for sure. Bronner's story was heard by so many, mainly because of *The Rick and Bubba Show*. The show has more than a million listeners, and Rick is sort of a local celebrity. It seemed everyone knew about what happened, from Focus on the Family in Colorado Springs to Fox News in New York. We received sympathy cards from across the country. Rick's message at Bronner's memorial service, taped by his co-worker, was the most-watched video on YouTube the week it was posted, and more

I know that a true child is empathetic toward a brokenhearted parent . . . because I have found that I, too, am the child of a brokenhearted parent.

than 620,000 people have watched it to the date I am writing now. Rick has received countless emails from people who were touched by that message, including a man writing from jail who told Rick he gave his life to the Lord because of it. It shouldn't surprise us that a criminal can relate to the pain caused by the absence of a beloved child, for he certainly could be no stranger to brokenness and loss. Without question, the hope of a new beginning with Christ shines brightly even through prison bars.

I personally took the message all the way to India on a missions trip to work with women who had been rescued from the sex trade, and I could see it in their eyes. They sympathized . . . with me. They, who had been dealt the worst of cards, were sympathetic toward me. Like Rick said, "There's just something special about a child" that moves people. They know that baby is innocent, and they know they're not. They want to know, as Rick's rugged, football-coach dad did, why God couldn't have taken somebody who actually deserved it. He will, Pop. He will. But for now, it had to be Bronner. The youngest, the most helpless, the sweetest, and the most innocent. It couldn't have been you, Pop. It had to be Bronner. That would be the most shocking. On first look, you would think it the most cruel loss, but maybe not, maybe just the most effective. Blake and Pop probably had similar thoughts. Blake looked at the picture of Bronner beside him on his high school football field as they ran together after a game and said, "He was so small next to me." They were both angry at first, but over time they began to see what everyone else could see—the good.

Men sometimes struggle with God more than women, I think, because most women know they need something beyond themselves, a protector, a provider, a husband, a Father. Men tend to think of themselves in reference to their own strength. Nothing can harm them, they believe, because if anyone or anything comes against them, they can defend themselves. They don't need anybody or anything to provide for them; they can provide for themselves. It's a man's strength that gets in the way of God many, many times. Rick said that the first day he had to go back to work after all this happened was a day of revelation about this very thing. Work, he said, had always been second nature to him, but not on this day:

> It was winter, and I was sitting in the dark trying to put my boots on to go to work. And I just couldn't muster the strength to tie them. I prayed, "Lord, I can't go. How can You expect me to go on the air and do a show when I can't even tie my boot strings?" I heard a response in my spirit that was so clear. "Now you're ready. Your problem isn't that you aren't strong enough; your problem is that you weren't weak enough. You are totally dependent upon Me to even tie your shoes. Now I can work through you like never before."

> *At that time the disciples came to Jesus, saying, "Who is the greatest in the kingdom of heaven?" And calling to Him a child, he put him in the midst of them and said, "Truly, I say to you, unless you turn and become like children, you will never enter the kingdom of heaven. Whoever humbles himself like this child is the greatest in the kingdom of heaven."*
>
> —MATTHEW 18:1–4

It's His strength we need. It's His Spirit we need. We can't do it alone. Life is too hard for a mere man, no matter how big and strong he thinks he is. We need God, all of us, from the biggest and most powerful, to the weakest and the smallest.

"Not by might, nor by power, but by my Spirit, says the LORD of hosts" (*Zechariah 4:6*).

I distinctly remember telling Blake at the memorial service, "Now the four of you will have to accomplish what five would have." I didn't know then how much Bronner would go out ahead of us all in bringing people to a deeper understanding of God, myself included. It was a stupid thing to say to Blake, I know. But he sort of heard me, I think. He went on to play football at Auburn University, knowing it would make his dad and his Pop so very proud, and it did. They are big football people — playing it, coaching it, watching it. Pop even has a football field named after him. The whole thing was good for our family. It gave us something to cheer about, watching Blake go all the way to a national championship. It was great, and he knew it. I believe Blake did that as much for his family as he did for himself. And it helped.

Brody was the closest in age to Bronner and played with him the most, certainly. He was so young and full of faith and trust, but I could see a little of his shine go dim after that dark day. He would have been the best big brother ever. He adored Bronner and doted on him all the time. Bronner even tried to get away from him sometimes, as if he didn't want to be smothered by all of Brody's attention. So I have often mourned the fact that Brody doesn't get to be a big brother, although he really still is Bronner's big brother but not in the way he would have been. Little things Brody said told me just how much he missed Bronner. We took a trip to Israel on the first anniversary of Bronner's heaven going. It was a missions trip, but it was so much more than that. Brody asked me, as we were waiting for our international flight to depart, if I thought the plane might

And, maybe for the first time ever, I began to feel compassion for God.

crash. I told him that I didn't think it would, that I believed God wanted us to see His homeland, that He had something special to show us there, in Israel. Brody said, "But it might," with notes of happiness and hope in his tone. He wanted to see Bronner again. And on one of Bronner's would-be birthdays, Rick asked the boys if they could imagine Bronner at that age, and Brody said, "Yes, I can; he would be my best buddy."

But Brooks had the most extreme reaction of all. Rick and I were walking around the pond just talking, grieving, in those first few days at the farm, and Brooks was walking along at a distance behind us. He was looking at the ground deep in thought when he started walking into the pond. It was still January. I turned around to see him doing this and yelled, "Brooks, what are you doing? Get out of the water!"

He said, "I want to drown; I want to do it for Bronner."

I said, "Brooks, you can't do that to me! I've already lost one son; I can't lose another!"

I tried to explain to him that things won't always be like this, that we would all be together again one day as a family. There were these old farm dogs down there. They were just neighborhood dogs, and they were always around. I said, "Look at those dogs. When Jesus comes back, that dog won't have a bad leg, and that one won't have a bad eye. Things aren't perfect right now, but they will be. One day, you're going to get to pet a lion, and it won't bite you. Jesus is going to make everything right and good and perfect one day, even the animals."

I could see his wheels turning. He got it. He understood, but even still, he would nestle close beside me on the couch sometime later and tell me how he wished it had been him so that I would "still have Bronner to snuggle." He saw how brokenhearted I was, which broke his heart even more. What Christlikeness from a then nine-year-old boy who loved his mother so much that he would be willing to lay down his life if that's what it would take to make her happy again.

Oh, my sweet Brooks, I would have been just as brokenhearted if it had been you.

He had seen me every day with Bronner, how I fussed over and loved on and snuggled him. Maybe in Brooks's eyes, I loved Bronner more. Maybe the baby seemed the most special to me, but Brooks, he was only smaller. That's all. I'm sorry I ever made you feel that way. I know you need me, too, and you are enough for me. You and your daddy and your brothers and your sister . . . you're enough. You are all worth fighting for, worth living for, and I will. I will. I will fight for you, all of you, and I will lay down my life for Him, for the great treasure of His presence forevermore.

> For to me to live is Christ, and to die is gain. If I am to live in the flesh, that means fruitful labor for me . . . My desire is to depart and be with Christ, for that is far better. But to remain in the flesh is more necessary on your account. Convinced of this, I know that I will remain and continue with you all, for your progress and joy in the faith, so that in me you may have ample cause to glory in Christ Jesus, because of my coming to you again. Only let your manner of life be worthy of the gospel of Christ.
>
> —PHILIPPIANS 1:21–27

They asked me about it one day, whether I loved Bronner more. I was putting every picture I could find of Bronner in a frame so I could see his little face everywhere. They wanted to know why. I told them that I still have them to look at; I needed pictures to see Bronner. But I also explained to them that a mother's heart gets bigger with each child. When I married Rick, Brandi and Blake each got their own special spot in my heart, and when I had Brooks, he took his place in my heart. It wasn't Brandi's part or Blake's. They had their own love from me, but this love would be for Brooks alone. The same happened for Brody and then for Bronner. Bronner never took one ounce of my love away from anyone else; he had his own.

I think the same is true of God: God's love for each person is his or hers alone. My relationship with God is so personal, so one-on-one. It's hard to imagine that He has that kind of relationship with so many other people, but when I think about it in the way that I love my own children in their own unique way, I get it. Brooks is like no other. Brody is like no other. Brandi, Blake, Bronner . . . all so unique, so special, so perfectly themselves. When I say, "I love you," I mean it. *You* . . . all of you. You are so special to me. You, Brooks. You, Brody. You, Brandi. You, Blake. And you, Bronner, every bit of you! I love *you*, perfect you! You, Brooks, may not be Bronner, but you are mine just the same. I believe that's how God feels about His children. We're His, and He loves each of us with our own unconditional, unique, personal, and perfect love.

And for all the rest who haven't yet claimed their place in the family of God, He waits for you. His heart is big enough for everyone, and He invites you, even now, to take the part in His heart's home that was created just for you.

"But to all who did receive him, who believed in his name, he gave the right to become children of God, who were born, not of blood nor of the will of the flesh nor of the will of man, but of God" (John 1:12–13).

I know that a true child is empathetic toward a brokenhearted parent not only because my own son told me with conviction that he would have willingly taken Bronner's place for my sake but also because I have found that I, too, am the child of a brokenhearted parent.

As Rick had to go back to work, the boys and Brandi had to go back to school. Brandi drove herself, as I've said, to the Alabama School of Fine Arts, and I drove Brooks and Brody each morning to their elementary school. I would stop by our house in Indian Springs to check the mail and water the many houseplants sent to the church for the memorial service. I sometimes lingered and went through the snapshots I had taken of Bronner's life with me, and friends would occasionally catch me there and sit beside me and share in my memories of him. I usually stopped by Bronner's grave to pray and to grieve, and then I drove the long way back to the farm alone. Rick would pick the boys up from school each afternoon before heading back there himself. I guess I wanted to protect Brooks and Brody from the memory of that night. I kept them away from there, hoping to make new memories somewhere else until the tenderness of their wounded hearts began to heal.

One day, I opened the mailbox to find a book. People sent many books, letters, cards, and they all helped. Most of the books were about grief, theological books, some were even about sheep and shepherds, books on hope and peace and

And for all the rest who haven't yet claimed their place in the family of God, He waits for you.

heaven. But this particular book surprised me, I guess. I turned it over in my hand and started reading the back cover. It was written by a pastor at a church somewhere I can't recall. He went to such and such seminary. He had a wife. I can't remember her name. They had four children, and one of them "had gone on to be with the Lord." As I read those words, I burst into tears. I wasn't expecting it. I don't know why. I should have. I guess I thought it would be a theological explanation for pain and suffering or something along those lines. But it wasn't that. This pastor's son had drowned just like mine had. I know, because I had written it in my prayer journal very early on, that I trusted and believed from the very beginning that God knew there was no other way than this, but my mother's heart cried out that day for the children.

"Why the children? Why, God? Why would you take the children? Why this pastor's son when he had given his life in service to You? Why me who loved Bronner and wanted him? I wanted him! There is nothing worse than losing a child! Nothing! I know You lost Your Son, but You got Him back after three days! Three days!"

And I felt a gentle stirring in my spirit. "But what about the others? They're *all* Mine. You're going to get a glorious reunion with your son, but I won't get that with all of Mine."

I got it. I understood. In stunned silence, I lowered my face from looking up at Him to question Him in His ways, and I realized only then, in that moment, that there is something much worse than having a child in heaven. And, maybe for the first time ever, I began to feel compassion for God. He, because of His own holiness, must send away from His presence so many He longs to save.

"O Jerusalem, Jerusalem . . . How often I wanted to gather your children together, as a hen gathers her chicks under her wings, but you were not willing!" (Matthew 23:37 NKJV).

"Jesus wept," the Bible says, in John 11:35, not only for Jerusalem that should have been His hometown but wasn't, but also for His friend, Lazarus, who had died. He must have known He was going to raise him from among the dead, but He still cried. Why?

I believe Jerusalem and Lazarus were just points on a compass. They represented the whole world—the fallen state of man. Jesus knew what was meant for the world, the intent for which it was created, and look how far it had fallen. The holy city that was to be a mirror image of the Holy City above wasn't holy at all. It was just like everybody else, and everybody else was depraved. Lazarus, though a friend of Jesus, died just like everybody else. And so Jesus wept. It is sad. People were created for God, to have fellowship with Him, to know Him, and to be with Him, but people run to and fro within the earth, and they forget that. They forget God. And I believe that breaks His heart.

Human willfulness runs deep and cuts to the heart of God. In Revelation, we see the kings of the earth, generals, great, powerful people hiding in caves and among the rocks of the mountains, but instead of calling out to God for forgiveness and mercy as even then He would so freely give, they cry out to the mountains and the rocks themselves, asking them to hide them from "the face of him who is seated on the throne, and from the wrath of the Lamb, for the great day of their wrath has come, and who can stand?" (Revelation 6:16–17). They know exactly what is happening to them and from whose hand it comes, but in their willfulness, they still won't submit to Him. They hold fast to their own grip of death in defiance of God.

God does not delight in this. He does not delight in death, real death, the kind that sends souls away from their Maker forever. My broken heart must surely pale in comparison to His. Love, Himself, rejected, crucified. A Father's way of salvation scoffed at, discarded. Help and comfort scorned. People making a way for themselves. It is His very breath we breathe, all of us, the breath of life. We should all be His, but we're not. We have each gone our own way. We've turned our backs on God. Lost but not forgotten.

I knew then that this wasn't about me. It was about Him. He wanted Bronner and Rick and me to be used as instruments to help bring some of His own back home to Him, to His heart's home. And I say, "Yes, Lord. I know it's not just me You love. There are so many others waiting to hear. If by my temporary sacrifice others can and will have an eternity with You, I submit. You have shown me Your light and Your salvation. You have given me Your love. If now, You want to use me to show others that light and salvation, I can say, yes. You are the Potter; I, but clay."

> *Enter by the narrow gate. For the gate is wide and the way is easy that leads to destruction, and those who enter by it are many. For the gate is narrow and the way is* hard *that leads to life, and those who find it are* few.
> —MATTHEW 7:13–14, AUTHOR'S EMPHASIS

I realized then on that day that God, in taking my baby from me for a time, a season, meant to bring some of His back to Himself for eternity.

Jesus taught this parable:

> *What man of you, having a hundred sheep, if he has lost one of them, does not leave the ninety-nine in the open country, and go after the one that is lost, until he finds it? And when he has found it, he lays it on his shoulders, rejoicing. And when he comes home, he calls together his friends and his neighbors, saying to them, "Rejoice with me, for I have found my sheep that was lost." Just so, I tell you, there will be more joy in heaven over one sinner who repents than over ninety-nine righteous persons who need no repentance.*
> —LUKE 15:4–7

I can understand the importance of *one* who is missing. What if that sheep weren't a sheep but a child, a baby, one you had carried in your womb for 40 weeks and nursed for eight months and dreamed about all of your life and once held in your arms you could never let go of without a fight? Who wouldn't move heaven and earth for *one* so loved as long as you knew you could put it all back together in the end? I have other children, yes, but they have their own love and their own space in my heart. Bronner's belongs to Bronner alone. I am glad for the others, and they are worth living for. They are worthy of my love and my time. They are beautiful, grand, exceptional people that I am so thankful for, but they are not Bronner.

So I understand that when God has my heart and Rick's heart and so many others, it's not enough. He wants *all* who belong to Him. It's not just me He loves; it's you, dear reader, and everyone you know or don't know. It's His breath we breathe, the breath of life. We should all be His, but we're not because we've turned our backs on God. We don't listen for His voice, so we don't hear Him when He speaks. We have enthroned ourselves to rule and to reign over our own lives, and we have forgotten who gave us our lives in the first place. He is the giver of life and the wellspring from which it comes, and when we are bound up in His life, as C. S. Lewis put it, how could we do anything but live forever? But "Once a man is separated from God, what can he do but wither and die?" I'm not—we're not—talking about biological life. I'm talking about forever. I'm talking about eternity. We're all dying here in this valley of the shadow of death that first was cast upon it by God Himself as He killed the animals to clothe those whose nakedness had just been realized. God showed Adam and Eve long ago what must be done to atone for their sin. It was just an animal there in the garden, but it would be so much more when the final sacrifice would be made to pay for the sins of the world. God taught Moses that the sacrificial lamb must be a male without blemish. Yes, an animal at first, but all of it points to Jesus, God incarnate, made manifest in the earth by the power of the Holy Spirit.

He, in the living and the dying, was everything we needed to get "into" God, or rather let His Spirit come into us and make us alive, alive in the Spirit, for we're more than flesh. It's the spirit part of us that makes us like our Creator who is, and who was, and is to come. He has no ending. He has no beginning. To live in Him is to set our minds on life and peace. Apart from Him, we die, as I would put it to my current seventh grade Sunday School class, a forever death.

> *There is therefore now no condemnation for those who are in Christ Jesus. For the law of the Spirit of life has set you free in Christ Jesus from the law of sin and death. For God has done what the law, weakened by the flesh, could not do. By sending his own Son in the likeness of sinful flesh and for sin, he condemned sin in the flesh, in order that the righteous requirement of the law might be fulfilled in us, who walk not according to the flesh but according to the Spirit. For those who live according to the flesh set their minds on the things of the flesh, but those who live according to the Spirit set their minds on the things of the Spirit. For to set the mind on the flesh is death, but to set the mind on the Spirit is life and peace.*
>
> —ROMANS 8:1–6

Jesus went on to say,

> *Or what woman, having ten silver coins, if she loses one coin, does not light a lamp and sweep the house and seek diligently until she finds it? And when she has found it, she calls together her friends and neighbors, saying, "Rejoice with me, for I have found the coin that I lost."*

Just so, I tell you, there is joy before the angels of God over
one sinner who repents.

—Luke 15:8–10

I know there will be those even among God's elect who will scoff at the nature of the communication and intimacy my husband and I had with God during this great time of grief and pain. I've heard it said that all we need of God is already written, and that may be true for some. But I ask, who was the one Jesus appeared to first but the one who stood outside His tomb, grief-stricken and weeping?

God's compassion runs deep for those He loves. There is no one alive today who loves God's Word more than I do, but God was there for me in my despair. He rescued me from danger. I am held in the grip of His great grace and in the power of His Resurrection. You can't think your way to God. This is a matter of the heart. Or maybe you haven't lived long enough to be tested in the great depths of God's waves. Wait. If your faith is really real, it will be tested.

Be wretched and mourn and weep. Let your laughter be
turned to mourning and your joy to gloom. Humble your-
selves before the Lord, and he will exalt you.

—James 4:9–10

How long, O simple ones, will you love being simple?
How long will scoffers delight in their scoffing and fools
hate knowledge?

—Proverbs 1:22

But if, by chance, God ever tells me anything I can't confirm in Scripture, I'll know it's not from Him.

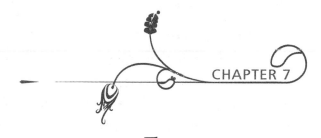

FAITH—TESTED, GENUINE, AND PRECIOUS

God said to Abram, "Go," and he went. No questions asked.

Then the Bible says the word of the Lord came to Abram in a vision.

The word of the Lord? That's Jesus. "In the beginning was the Word, and the Word was with God, and Word was God (John 1:1).

"He is the image of the invisible God" (Colossians 1:15).

Indeed, Jesus Himself could be the only reconciliation for these two statements from Exodus 33: "Thus the LORD used to speak to Moses face to face, as a man speaks to his friend" (v. 11), and, "You cannot see my face, for man shall not see me and live" (v. 20).

In Genesis 18, we see the Lord not only visiting and talking with Abraham but also eating the food of his household as Abraham stood by Him under the shade of the oaks of Mamre. Who but Jesus could do this? Not the Father and not the Spirit. This is Jesus. It is but a foretaste of the breakfast that the resurrected Christ would prepare for His broken disciples by the Sea of Tiberias just before telling Simon Peter three times to feed the flock of His pasture. To understand this is significant because it reveals the oneness of God's character and the great height of His ways. The God of the

Old Testament is the God of the New. The fire and the pillar of cloud, the fierce defender of His people, the refiner, the One who set life and death and great commandments before the Israelites is the same God who cleared the temple and chastised the Pharisees and who humbled Himself even unto death upon the Cross of Calvary so that we who would believe could live.

"Jesus Christ is the same yesterday and today and forever" (Hebrews 13:8).

So the preincarnate Christ appears to Abram in theophany and says to him: "Fear not, Abram, I am your shield; your reward shall be very great" (Genesis 15:1).

Reward for what?

Obedience. For going when he was told to go. Jesus said, "If you love me, you will keep my commandments" (John 14:15). Abram showed his love for God by his obedience to God.

And, so do we. Jesus again declares, "Whoever has my commandments and keeps them, he it is who loves me" (v. 21). And again Jesus answers, "If anyone loves me, he will keep my word, and my Father will love him, and we will come to him and make our home with him. Whoever does not love me does not keep my words" (vv. 23–24). Again and again Jesus touts obedience as evidence of true devotion.

So when God appears to Abram and says that his reward would be great, Abram wants to know what God could give him that would be better than his very own son. He's asking. He wants a son for his very own. That was his heart's desire. And God said, "OK, I'll give you what you want and so much more." He brought him outside to look at the stars and said, "Count them, if you can, that's how many your offspring will be."

Can you imagine how big his eyes must have gotten? That's a "wow moment" right there. When God comes down from heaven and shows you the future, your future, and it is very bright. Wow!

And Abram believed it. The Bible says that Abram believed the Lord, and that belief, that faith and trust in God, was counted to him as righteousness.

"And he believed the LORD, and he counted it to him as righteousness" (Genesis 15:6).

I don't just believe in Him anymore. I love Him. Rick and I love the Lord. We have an intimacy with God that came through our suffering.

The righteousness of God has always come by faith, and faith has always come by the word of the Lord. It "is the assurance of things hoped for, the conviction of things not seen" (Hebrews 11:1). The sure belief that what I hope for will come to pass, even if I can't see any evidence for it, and yet being completely convinced that that which I can't see is real . . . that's faith.

"In all circumstances take up the shield of faith, with which you can extinguish all the flaming darts of the evil one" (Ephesians 6:16).

Now, Abram's wife was barren. There had been no evidence up to that point that she could bear him a son, but when God told him it would happen, Abram believed it. He believed that he would receive what he hoped for, a son. He believed God, and God counted it to him as righteousness.

Stop right here. If Abram had died right then and there, he would have gone to heaven because his faith had saved him.

The Apostle Paul tells us in Romans 3:22–25 that "the righteousness of God" comes "through faith in Jesus Christ for all who believe." He says that yes, "all have sinned and fall short of the glory of God," but through faith we can stand justified before the Lord. That's why he calls it grace. Grace is a free gift. Yes, we've sinned but we're counted as righteous. The gift is righteousness. And everyone who believes by faith can receive the gift, a gift based solely on the grace of God. Our own righteousness apart from faith is like filthy rags compared to the righteousness of God because "in him is no darkness at all" (1 John 1:5). But He clothes us in His light, in His righteousness. As we've seen from the Book of Revelation in our Bible, God longs to literally clothe us in white garments. He takes away our filthy rags and clothes us in fine linen, bright and pure.

But Abram didn't die right then, did he? God had more for him. He did give him that son, a son brought forth from an aged, barren woman of 90, and the son of promise was born. They called him Isaac, which means laughter, because they were so happy. They were so happy and blessed because they had a baby, a son, their very own son.

Abram became Abraham because Abraham means father of a multitude. God told him that through him and through his offspring all nations of the earth would be blessed.

Again . . . wow! What a great moment in time for the father of our faith, Abraham.

But look what comes next.

Genesis 22:1 says, "After these things God tested Abraham."

God tested Abraham. He tested his faith, his trust and hope in Him, not to see for Himself which way Abraham would go because God knew what Abraham would do, but God was building Abraham up into his most holy faith. Abraham had already shown that he had faith in God, but then God tested him in order to grow his faith, to refine it, to build it up.

Saving faith can be as small as a mustard seed. Have you ever seen a mustard seed? It's small. The smallest of all seeds, Jesus taught in the parable, but when it's watered and cultivated and tended it grows to be the largest of all garden plants. It becomes a tree. That's how God wants our faith to grow, to get bigger and greater and more holy until it's like a great big tree that can't be shaken from its roots, the roots of faith.

Faith can be added to and supplemented.

In fact, 2 Peter 1:5–7 tells us to "*Make every effort* to supplement your faith with virtue, and virtue with knowledge, and knowledge with self-control, and self-control with steadfastness, and steadfastness with godliness, and godliness with brotherly affection, and brotherly affection with love" (author's emphasis), which binds it all "together in perfect harmony" (Colossians 3:14).

And what do you think Abraham was tested with?

His son, of course, the one thing in life that meant the most to him, what he had waited a lifetime for, the son of promise, through whom all of those future blessings were supposed to come.

Isaac.

God told Abraham to take his son, "Your only son Isaac, whom you love, and go to the land of Moriah, and offer him there as a burnt offering on one of the mountains of which I shall tell you" (Genesis 22:2).

God, the Father, wanted Abraham to be like Himself, who would also offer His Son, His only Son, Jesus, whom He loved, on the altar of sacrifice.

Look at what godliness Abraham exemplifies here in this moment: He got up early in the morning, the Bible says, saddled his donkey, got some wood—He even had Isaac carry it—and he walked with his son up Mount Moriah.

Why would he do it? Why?

Because he trusted in God. He believed Him. His faith never wavered.

Hebrews 11:19 explains that Abraham considered and took into mind the fact "that God was able even to raise him from the dead." That's what God did with His own Son, Jesus. He raised Him from the dead. Abraham knew He could. Abraham also knew that God was his friend, that God loved him, and that God was good, not evil. So he knew that even if he did sacrifice Isaac, it wouldn't be the end of Isaac. Because Abraham knew that in God, there is life everlasting.

Now, I'm the one saying, "Wow!" Wow, Father Abraham, you never even hesitated. You never once even asked why. You just believed in God. Wow!

When God asked me for my son, my baby, I had a lot of questions, but glory and praise and honor be to God because He answered every one of them.

God took away my son for the same reason He asked Abraham to sacrifice his, to enlarge my faith, to look not to this world as my home but beyond this life and this world, to heaven where Bronner is. The things that I can't see have become just as or more important than what I can see. The things of the Spirit, the things that can't be grasped and touched, the future, a future in which I, like Abraham, will walk down off that mount with my son by my side, my one and only Bronner, my baby. And everything I hope for will become my reality.

I can't see Bronner anymore. I can't hold him or touch him or kiss his soft cheek. He was taken from me in an instant, in a flash of horror, sudden calamity that I never expected nor could I have antici- pated. But I know it's not forever. I know with perfect assurance that I

If I'm not making faith in God seem very attractive with all the sifting of the wheat and the pressing of the oil, I'm just going to go old school on you for a minute: What other choice do we have? Satan? Hell? Eternal condemnation and separation from God? Umm . . . no thanks! I'll take the faith with a double helping of the Cross and a little pain and suffering to go with it.

will see him again, and more than that, I am completely convinced that my sacrifice of time with him now has been used to build upon the foundation of Christ a great temple of praise that when revealed by fire will shine like refined gold among the rarest and most costly of jewels.

It was Abraham's great faith that brought him to the test, and when he had stood the test, God reaffirmed to Abraham what He had known all along, that in Abraham's offspring, all the nations of the earth would be blessed. That blessing would be made manifest in the person of Jesus Christ, who would draw people from every tongue, tribe, and nation.

✱ *"And I, when I am lifted up from the earth, will draw all people to myself" (John 12:32).*

God wants us to know Him more, to love Him more, to build ourselves up in our most holy faith. One day at church, we were singing, and Rick, in this moment of sheer awe and worship and love for the Lord, looked at me and said, "I can't *believe* I've ever sinned against Him." God takes away his son, and he responds with, "I can't believe I've ever sinned against Him."

You want to grow your faith? Let it start out small, and allow God to cultivate it into an oak of righteousness that can never be shaken, no matter what. Come hell or high water, don't ever let go of the one who pulled you up out of the darkness in the first place. And when that time comes, don't be afraid; just believe.

✱*"Trust in the LORD with all your heart and lean not on your own understanding" (Proverbs 3:5 NIV).*

Trust in the Lord with all your heart and lean not on your own understanding. . . .

Trust in the Lord with all your heart and lean not on your own understanding.

I can't tell you how many times I said this to myself. Over and over would I repeat it . . . trying to let it sink in. It may not make sense at first, whatever the trial or test may be, but God is able to make us see that our sufferings produce in us endurance, and endurance character, and character hope.

"Now hope that is seen is not hope. For who hopes for what he sees? But if we hope for what we do not see, we wait for it with patience" (Romans 8:24–25).

Just as Abraham trusted in God's promise, so do I. I believe that Bronner is safe with God in heaven. I believe all things, and I will endure all things because I know in whom I have believed. I have believed in a God who can be trusted, a God who loves me so much that he would give up His Son, too . . . for me.

You want your faith to be strengthened? Grow it until it becomes love. I don't just believe in Him anymore. I love Him. Rick and I love the Lord. We have an intimacy with God that came through our suffering. I know Him. He's not only my Savior; He's my friend and my Father and my Helper all wrapped up in One. He's everything. I know that without Him I am nothing and can do nothing.

Without Him, I would have no hope of ever seeing my son again. But I do hope . . . I have all the hope in the world because I know in whom I have believed, and He is good. He is good. He loves me so much that He would sacrifice His Son for me. Abraham proved himself godly by his willingness to do what God was willing to do, sacrifice his son. Abraham was willing to do it for God because He trusted in God. God did it for love. He did it to redeem us. His holiness requires justice, a propitiation for sin, and He was willing to pay it because even if "we esteemed Him not" (Isaiah 53:3), He esteems us. He deems us valuable, worthy of the price He would pay, and no one, no thing can ever take that away.

And now I know how great my faith really was that He should allow me to be tested in such a way. A natural-born person would think I'm crazy, but a person born of the Spirit understands. Thank You, Lord, for trusting me with something so great that I would be asked to give up what you gave up: a son.

When we were in Israel, we saw ancient olive presses. They are these big stone containers that kind of look like a doughnut with the middle part rising up so that there is a ring where they would place the olives. Then there's a larger stone that would be pressed down over the olives to crush them. This is the first step in collecting the precious golden oil contained in that fruit. The second step is very similar, the gathering of the crushed olives into baskets and pressing them further still until all that is left is a refined, glorious oil used for the anointing of priests and prophets and kings, for the lighting of lamps, and for daily food.

Our word *Christ* comes from the Greek word *christos*, meaning "anointed one," covered in oil. The oil is the Spirit of God, the Holy Spirit. It is God's Spirit alone who could bring such beauty and gladness from something so crushed. Only He could bring life back from the bleak depths of darkness and death, and He has and He does and He will.

> If the Spirit of him who raised Jesus from the dead dwells in you, he who raised Christ Jesus from the dead will also give life to your mortal bodies through his Spirit who dwells in you. So then, brothers, we are debtors, not to the flesh, to live according to the flesh. For if you live according to the flesh you will die, but if by the Spirit you put to death the deeds of the body, you will live. For all who are led by the Spirit of God are sons of God. For you did not receive the spirit of slavery to fall back into fear,

but you have received the Spirit of adoption as sons, by whom we cry, "Abba! Father!" The Spirit himself bears witness with our spirit that we are children of God, and if children, then heirs — heirs of God and fellow heirs with Christ, provided we suffer with him in order that we may also be glorified with him.

—ROMANS 8:11–17

God's Spirit is indeed strong, but He is also gentle and kind. It was in the form of a dove that the Holy Spirit descended upon Jesus at His baptism, for He is both powerful and pure. His strength surpasses that of an army of angels, but His comfort is as personal and as peaceful as the sweetest song of heaven. Yes, we must suffer with Christ in order to be glorified with Him, but He has not left us alone in this world. He has given us of His Spirit to help us and to kiss our face like a gentle breeze with His love. The olive presses we saw in Capernaum were filled with meaning for us. We felt that we, too, had been crushed under the rock that is Christ, but we knew, however painful, that He meant only to squeeze out the worldliness, self-reliance, and pride from our lives because only then would we become dependent upon God for our very breath. And *that* is what He desires of us all.

✱ "The sacrifices of God are a broken spirit; a broken and contrite heart, O God, you will not despise" (Psalm 51:17).

It is not in a man or a woman to rule himself or herself justly. Only God can do that. He alone is just. He alone is righteous. He alone is good. And, might I add, only He knows the future. We have to trust Him because He alone sees it all, the big picture, how He weaves everything together into one perfect tapestry of life. He guards our feet from stumbling and puts us on right paths. We grapple in the dark, even as He longs to bring us into His glorious light. The sin nature in us is one of lordship and authority over ourselves. It is in our very nature to want to be God. It was Lucifer's downfall, and it is ours as well. But we aren't God, none of us. We are all created beings. None of us can boast eternal existence. Each of us has a beginning, and our beginning is with God. Let's let our life's story end with Him as well. Satan will most assuredly come to sift us like wheat in this world, and when he does, let's let ourselves become bread upon the table of God.

"Jesus said to them, 'My food is to do the will of him who sent me and to accomplish his work . . . Look, I tell you, lift up your eyes, and see that the fields are white for harvest'" (John 4:34–35).

January is truly the darkest and the coldest of months, but the promise of an eternal spring anchors my soul through the deepest of winters.

If I'm not making faith in God seem very attractive with all the sifting of the wheat and the pressing of the oil, I'm just gonna go old school on you for a minute: What other choice do we have? Satan? Hell? Eternal condemnation and separation from God?

Umm . . . no thanks! I'll take the faith with a double helping of the Cross and a little pain and suffering to go with it. Because the pain will end for those who believe.

To borrow a concept from C. S. Lewis: the earth is all of heaven that some people will ever know, but for those of faith, it will be the only hell we will ever know. In the preface of *The Great Divorce*, Lewis writes, "I think earth, if chosen instead of Heaven, will turn out to have been, all along, only a region in Hell: and earth, if put second to Heaven, to have been from the beginning a part of Heaven itself." We live in a fallen creation. Death entered into the world through sin,

Our beginning is with God. Let's let our life's story end with Him as well.

and death is bad. I know. I feel the pain of that separation every day, but I know . . . I *know* it's not forever. And I am eternally grateful that this is the worst of hell I will ever know.

✱ *"And after you have suffered a little while, the God of all grace, who has called you to his eternal glory in Christ, will himself restore, confirm, strengthen, and establish you" (1 Peter 5:10).*

Have faith in God, and then let your faith grow by any means possible all the way until it becomes love, love for God and love for others. This is the most excellent way. Jesus said the first and greatest commandment is to "Love the Lord your God with all your heart and with all your soul and with all your mind . . . And a second is like it: You shall love your neighbor as yourself"✱(Matthew 22:37–39).

This was the way it was always supposed to be. The commandment came because of sin. God had to command us to love Him and to obey Him, which is really sad because He's our Father. We should naturally love and obey Him, have respect for Him, trust Him, but we don't. Our sin nature is too strong. But small beginnings can have great endings. Faith as small as a mustard seed can grow into a great tree filled with love and devotion to God and to others. And then nothing will ever be able to separate us "from the love of God in Christ Jesus our Lord" (Romans 8:39).

Water and the Spirit

Bronner went to heaven by way of water. I have always considered it his baptism. But instead of Danny raising him up "to walk in newness of life" as he did with the other four children, Jesus raised him up. Brandi, Blake, and Brooks were all baptized in the baptismal pool at Shades Mountain Baptist Church in Vestavia Hills, Alabama, but Bronner and Brody were baptized in the pool in our backyard. We saw Brody's baptism, a little more than three months after Bronner's, as a sort of taking back. We put on the invitations, sent to a small number of friends and family, this verse of Scripture: "Do not be overcome by evil, but overcome evil with good" (Romans 12:21). And we meant it. We were determined to live by that rule. We would, we have, and we will continue to overcome this great evil with ever greater good.

As I prepared for Brody's baptism that spring morning, I blew up white balloons to release at the end so that our eyes would be lifted heavenward. I placed Bible verses, prayers, and words of comfort and praise in each balloon. I blew up so many I couldn't get them through the door all at once, but I tried it anyway. One of the balloons popped, just one, and a Bible verse fell at my feet. It said, "The LORD will fight for you, and you have only to be silent"

✳ (Exodus 14:14). I believed it. I believe it still. I can feel Him fighting for me. He is the lifter of my head and the founder and the perfecter of my faith. I know that:

> ✳ *God is our refuge and strength, a very present help in trouble. Therefore we will not fear though the earth gives way, though the mountains be moved into the heart of the sea, though its waters roar and foam, though the mountains tremble at its swelling. There is a river whose streams make glad the city of God, the holy habitation of the Most High. God is in the midst of her; she shall not be moved; God will help her when morning dawns. The nations rage, the kingdoms totter; he utters his voice, the earth melts. The LORD of hosts is with us; the God of Jacob is our fortress. Come, behold the works of the LORD, how he has brought desolations on the earth. He makes wars cease to the end of the earth; he breaks the bow and shatters the spear; he burns the chariots with fire. "Be still, and know that I am God. I will be exalted among the nations, I will be exalted in the earth!" The LORD of hosts is with us; the God of Jacob is our fortress.*
>
> —PSALM 46

It is a great mystery to me that the earth itself was not only "formed out of water and through water by the word of God" (2 Peter 3:5), but it was also baptized with its own cleansing flood during the days of Noah. It is also interesting to note that my last name, and Rick's and Bronner's of course, is Burgess, which means "fortress" in at least one language: German. I may not be a mighty fortress, but I have one. His name is the Lord. His name is Jesus.

He came to John to be baptized by him. John protested and

said, "I need to be baptized by you, and do you come to me?" (Matthew 3:14). But Jesus assured John that it was fitting for Him to be baptized so that all righteousness would be fulfilled in Him. When Jesus went up from the water, the Spirit of God descended like a dove and came to rest upon Him, and a voice from heaven was heard saying, "This is my beloved Son, with whom I am well pleased" (Matthew 3:17). God, the Son, went down into the river Jordan and came up with God, the Holy Spirit, descending upon Him as God, the Father, confirmed Him as His own. The manifestation of God's triune nature in this baptismal scene is a rare occurrence in Scripture. For this reason, I believe baptism must be very holy in the sight of God.

John came baptizing with water but said that the One he came to proclaim would baptize us with the Holy Spirit and with fire. John's baptism was one of repentance for sin, and we know that the Lamb of God would take the sins of the world upon His shoulders bearing the weight of them on Calvary's Cross. Jesus came not only by water but also by blood, His own, as a reckoning or payment to cover our sins so that we may enter into the presence of a most holy God.

> *This is he who came by water and blood — Jesus Christ;*
> *not by the water only but by the water and the blood. And*
> *the Spirit is the one who testifies, because the Spirit is the*
> *truth. For there are three that testify: the Spirit and the*
> *water and the blood; and these three agree.*
>
> —1 JOHN 5:6–8

> *And this is the testimony, that God gave us eternal life,*
> *and this life is in his Son. Whoever has the Son has life;*
> *whoever does not have the Son of God does not have life.*
>
> —vv. 11–12

✳ Water represents repentance, the acknowledgement of one's own sinfulness coupled with the declaration to turn from it. Repentance does wipe the slate clean, but possibly even more than that, it declares that from that moment on, sin will no longer reign in us. The turning away from sin must be evident in our behavior, our speech, everything, and that is where the Spirit comes in. The Spirit helps us in our weakness, for He knows that change is hard and that the chains of sin don't break easily✳But Scripture says we must. ✳We must change if our repentance is real.

James, the Lord's brother, tells us in his epistle that those who claim Christ must reflect His Word. If not, he says we have deceived ourselves and are like someone who looks at himself in a mirror but as soon as he turns away has already forgotten what he looks like. He admonishes us not to be so mindless. "But the one who looks into the perfect law, the law of liberty, and perseveres, being no hearer who forgets but a doer who acts, he will be blessed in his doing" (James 1:25).

The turning away from sin becomes fruit born in us over time by God's own Spirit and is a lifelong process of sanctification. The marks of the Spirit in us are love and joy, peace and patience, kindness, goodness, faithfulness, gentleness, and self-control. I do not believe it a coincidence that among the fruit of the Spirit listed in ✳Galatians 5:22–23, self-control is listed last, for our sinful souls, although bought at a price and both forgiven and cleansed, are certainly hard to master. This is why Paul said he found it a law that whenever he wanted to do right, evil was always close at hand (Romans 7:21). So we must train ourselves for godliness in order to overrule the sinful nature implanted in us by our

We live in shadows upon the earth never fully grasping God's eternal glory, but we live by faith in what is to come.

ancestor, Adam. God warned Cain, the firstborn of Adam, about this very thing: "If you do well, will you not be accepted? And if you do not do well, sin is crouching at the door. Its desire is for you, but you must rule over it" (Genesis 4:7).

We must. Cain allowed jealousy, pride, and even hatred to fester inside his soul until it led him to murder his own brother, and when God gave him the opportunity to confess his sin, he not only lied about it but also showed not even the slightest trace of remorse. And then, the Bible says, Cain went away from the presence of the Lord. We must rule over the sin that still desires to have us even if we have been justified by faith and have made peace with God through our Lord Jesus Christ.

When God created man upon the earth, He created us, both male and female, in His own image (Genesis 1:27). The Bible tells us, "God is love" (1 John 4:8). So this hatred that led Cain to kill his brother, Abel, was the exact opposite of God's nature and image that must have still been born inside of him somewhere. But Cain let the sin nature take control and stamp out the love of God within his soul.

Imprints of the two natures left from the Garden of Eden remain in each of us. One was created in us from the beginning and bears the image of God, His goodness and His love. The other is bent toward sin. The two natures are so unalike that they naturally battle against each other. But when one is born of the Spirit by faith, he gets a Helper. It's like we get a double dose of the God nature when the Holy Spirit takes up residence in our hearts. It doesn't mean the battle isn't still on; it just means that now we can have the upper hand in the fight against sin and shame.

I am writing these things to you so that you may not sin.

—1 JOHN 2:1

Whoever says he abides in him ought to walk in the same way in which he walked.

—2:6

Everyone who makes a practice of sinning also practices lawlessness; sin is lawlessness. You know that he appeared in order to take away sins, and in him there is no sin. No one who abides in him keeps on sinning; no one who keeps on sinning has either seen him or known him. Little children, let no one deceive you. Whoever practices righteousness is righteous, as he is righteous. Whoever makes a practice of sinning is of the devil, for the devil has been sinning from the beginning. The reason the Son of God appeared was to destroy the works of the devil. No one born of God makes a practice of sinning, for God's seed abides in him, and he cannot keep on sinning because he has been born of God.

—3:4–9

Notice the wording here: "makes a practice of sinning." God knows that even His own will slip occasionally, but He tells us in His Word, "If we confess our sins, he is faithful and just to forgive us our sins and to cleanse us from all unrighteousness" (1 John 1:9). We can't, at once, claim to be enlightened by the truth of the gospel and also continue in habitual sin. The natural response to God's mercy and grace is one of adoration and the kind of gratitude that seeks to prove itself in a lifelong mission of obedience and service. Anything less than that must leave one wondering if he has been brought into the light of truth at all. Maybe he doesn't understand that he has been brought from death unto life, or maybe he just needs to work at taming his own flesh with self-control. Why is this so important? John makes his reasoning abundantly clear: "Abide in him, so that when he appears we may have confidence and not shrink from him in shame at his coming" (1 John 2:28).

Jesus is coming back, and John wants us to get the full effect of it. He knows there are some who have claimed Christ as Savior who will fall back into sin and will be found where they shouldn't be on that day of Christ's glorious appearing. When they see Him, instead of running to Him in exuberance, as they should, they'll "shrink from him in shame." Don't let that happen. Go for the "well done," as my husband likes to say. Rick says he can't wait to hear those words from his Savior and his Lord, Jesus Christ. So that's what we were doing on the day of Brody's baptism, that and so much more. We were standing with Christ and destroying the works of the devil, the very reason Christ came to the earth.

After Rick welcomed everyone, this is what I said on that momentous morning that our almost seven-year-old son was baptized:

> As Rick said, thank you so much for being here for us and for Brody. We love you all so much and are so glad to be sharing this wonderful event with you. Today, we'll be baptizing Brody, our fourth child, and that is so special; but we're doing something much greater here, as you all know. We're standing and not fainting, and that's a big deal. But we are also fighting the good fight and running the race.
>
> There is no greater privilege than to raise up children to be godly men and women. I was privileged to lead this young man, Brody, my son and my brother in Christ, in a prayer of salvation when he was five years old. That may

seem young to make such a big decision, but for Brody it was just a natural progression in the only life he has ever known. He has been immersed in the Holy Scripture since birth, just as Paul said of Timothy.

I remember Brody at three years old coming out of his Community Bible Study class and saying John 14:6 in its entirety, "I am the way, and the truth, and the life. No one comes to the Father except through me." Of course, I started crying. It just warmed my heart that he, at only three, could quote Scripture to me. That is the way it's supposed to be for Christian families. Children are so sweet, but they are capable of great faith. That's why Jesus said, "Unless you become like little children, you cannot enter the kingdom of heaven" (Matthew 18:3, author's paraphrase). They're humble, and they really believe. Let us all believe with that kind of faith, and let us humble ourselves like this little child who has come to this special place in his life.

I can't remember when Brody didn't just love and trust Jesus. So it was so "him" when we sat down at the table and were talking about our need for a Savior. I had drawn a picture for him of sinful man on one side, a cross in the middle, and Holy God on the other side. Brody said, "What am I doing over here with Satan? I'm gonna cross that bridge." And he did, so let's cross another bridge over the waters of this life and plunge beneath that cleansing flood to fulfill all righteousness, and as Ananias said to the soon to be Apostle Paul, "And now why do you wait? Rise and be baptized and wash away your sins, calling on his name" (Acts 22:16).

After the ceremony I found another small strip of paper lying in the backyard that must have fallen after one of the balloons popped in the pines. All it said was "love." *Love* had literally fallen from the sky that day. I have certainly felt God's love surrounding me, comforting me,

God is always at work in the world, even as He allows time for His plan and purpose to be played out in the earth.

assuring me in so many ways. Indeed, all of creation seemed to cry out with His comfort, like the day I sat by Bronner's grave, as I often did, and three little baby blue dragonflies danced around his gravestone. They immediately caught my attention because of their beautiful baby blue color, and I watched them curiously for a long time. I had never really noticed dragonflies before, but something about these reminded me of my little baby boy zipping about seemingly without a care in the world as happy as can be.

After that, I began noticing them everywhere, and they were always the baby blue ones. I saw them at our farm and at home around the pool, at Bronner's grave and at the fields where my boys played ball—it wasn't just a few here and there. I saw *hundreds* of them always and everywhere. I sensed they were from the Lord and had something to do with Bronner because they always made me think of him. "For all things are your servants" (Psalm 119:91). And, "The earth is the LORD's, and everything in it" (24:1 NIV).

I had heard of the symbolism of butterflies as they relate to the life, death, and Resurrection of Jesus. The caterpillar stage represents His earthly ministry; the chrysalis phase the tomb; and the last of winged beauty is likened unto His Resurrection. I even had a friend tell me that after her dad went to heaven, she kept seeing little yellow butterflies at odd junctures and in unusual ways and that over time she realized that God wanted her to know that we on earth are like a caterpillar, but her dad in heaven is like the fully developed butterfly. But God wasn't sending me butterflies, but dragonflies. I was perplexed. What did it mean? I didn't understand at all until after Brody's baptism.

If there were any remnants of death left in that pool, then surely it had been cleansed by Life Himself at such a reverent and beautiful and holy event as a young child's declaration that he belongs to the Lord forever. We felt that not only had Brody been sealed for the Lord that day but that we had done something more. We felt that we had taken our pool back for the purpose we built it in the first place, which certainly included fun and recreation, but also ministry. And so the kids started swimming in the pool again after the baptism. It was amazing to me to see them play as if nothing bad had ever happened there. They seemed as happy as ever splashing and playing games and jumping off the jumping rock and sliding down the slide, and I was glad and pensive as I stored it all up in my heart and treasured it.

Their resilience was a testament not only to their strength of character but also to their trust and zeal for the Lord. I had once told them, "You know the truth. You know Jesus, and that (Jesus) makes all the difference." And He had. That much was evident. So one day that May, Brandi, Brooks, Brody, and I were down by the pool swimming, and along came my beautiful baby blue dragonflies hanging around as if to join in the fun. One lit on the side of the pool, and as I approached it I saw that it had large, bulging green eyes and that the blue of its body was almost translucent with a shimmering gem-like quality about it. I thought it was

The joy is for what it will produce in us and in others, not the pain itself. It's OK to cry and to be mournful. There is a time for weeping.

absolutely stunning. It let me get so close that I was able to study it intently. It didn't move away from me for a long time.

I looked at the kids who knew all about the dragonflies I had been seeing and said, "OK, that's it! There is something going on with these dragonflies, and I'm going to find out what it is." I was beyond curious. Still wet from the pool, I searched the Internet to find out anything I could about dragonflies: what are they, where do they come from, and why are they called dragonflies? I didn't know a thing about dragonflies, but I was determined to learn. I searched out everything I could and then sat in stunned amazement at what I had learned, but truly only for a moment because I was so excited to tell the kids. I found out that a dragonfly goes through a metamorphosis just like a butterfly does, but a dragonfly's life begins in water.

Now that made sense to me. I believe God sent me the dragonflies to comfort me, to tell me that Bronner's life didn't end that night in the water. It began.

"Blessed are those who mourn, for they shall be comforted" *(Matthew 5:4).*

A dragonfly lays its eggs in the water. From the egg, something like a little water bug hatches. It's called a dragonfly nymph, and it lives in the water in this stage for up to three years. I understood that to mean that some could live as nymphs for two and a half years, which is kind of cool to think about, but when the dragonfly nymph is ready to move on to the next stage, he simply crawls out of the water on a reed or a stick. When the air touches its skin, it starts to breathe, and from a small slit in its back, the full-grown dragonfly emerges. As its wings unfurl, it will not take its initial flight at night. It waits for the morning. It waits for the light. A butterfly or a damselfly will sometimes close its wings together, but a dragonfly never does. It remains in the shape of a cross always.

There are more than 500 different kinds of dragonflies. They are found in a rainbow of colors and various sizes but always the same shape. The one I kept seeing, the one with a baby blue body and emerald green eyes, is called a *blue dasher*. Of course, a blue dasher! For what would be more appropriate for my little runner who dashed about at maximum speed everywhere he went? Of course, a blue dasher, for God knows better than I. He knows I would have never picked dragonflies as a comfort for myself, not because they aren't beautiful and colorful and vibrant creatures, but simply because of their name. I don't like dragons because I know that Satan is called a dragon, but I believe God did this so that I would know for sure that it wasn't of me or from me. I believe He did it because He loves me and wanted to assure me that Bronner is more alive now than ever before. Never once was there anything about this little blue insect that felt evil or wrong. It felt sweet and sure and perfect just like God and just like my love for Bronner. God wanted me to know for sure that Bronner has been born of both water and Spirit and that he lives with Him in a place where the River of Life flows through and Love Himself reigns.

"Jesus answered, 'Truly, truly, I say to you, unless one is born of water and the Spirit, he cannot enter the kingdom of God'" (John 3:5).

Bronner went to heaven by way of water and has been born into the paradise of God where he has entered into life.

There is a passage of Scripture from Matthew's Gospel that talks about entering life. It says,

> *Woe to the world for temptations to sin! For it is necessary that temptations come, but woe to the one by whom the temptation comes! And if your hand or foot causes*

*you to sin, cut it off and throw it away. It is better for
you to enter life crippled or lame than with two hands or
two feet to be thrown into the eternal fire. And if your eye
causes you to sin, tear it out and throw it away. It is better
for you to enter life with one eye than with two eyes to be
thrown into the hell of fire.*

—Matthew 18:7–9

I believe these words spoken by Jesus aren't to be taken as an instruction to literally cut off your hand or foot or to gouge out your eye but rather to crucify the sin in your life by taking away anything that may cause you to stumble such as a magazine subscription or an app on your phone. But that's not what stands out to me the most here. Those two little words, *enter life,* are the most meaningful to me. Jesus is comparing one thing to another here. One scenario ends in "hell" and an "eternal fire." The other is a place where we "enter life." He is certainly not talking about when we are first born because a newborn baby has no knowledge of sin or temptation. Neither does it seem that He is talking about the salvation experience in a believer, for a born-again Christian can certainly be tempted to sin. I believe what Jesus is talking about here is heaven. That is where we truly "enter life." It is where the Author of Life lives, and it is certainly the opposite of hell. We on earth can only get glimpses of the true life we will have there one day. We live in shadows upon the earth never fully grasping God's eternal glory, but we live by faith in what is to come.

Satan cannot take the wonder out of the earth, nor can he take it from our hearts. We live in hopeful anticipation, taking in everything we can of the Lord in the here and the now, knowing that there's so much more to come when we at last "enter life."

"The Spirit and the Bride say, 'Come.' And let the one who hears say, 'Come.' And let the one who is thirsty come; let the one who desires take the water of life without price" (Revelation 22:17).

SEVENS

Rick came into the kitchen to get me one morning from outside and said, "You've got to come see this." I walked out onto the deck and looked down toward the pool where he was pointing me and saw several doves sitting on the jumping rock. Our pool isn't deep enough for an actual diving board, so we had opted for a big rock the kids could jump into the pool from. As we moved closer to get a better view of them, the doves flew away all at once in a flutter of angelic beauty and grace. It wouldn't be the last time we would see the doves. They began nesting down by the pool and could be seen perching on the very tip top of our house. They continue there even today singing a mournful song that has become ever so familiar to us. The low coo of our mourning doves is a constant reminder that as we continue to grieve our baby boy, God mourns for and with us sending echoes of His love in every possible way.

> *Blessed be the God and Father of our Lord Jesus Christ,*
> *the Father of mercies and God of all comfort, who comforts*
> *us in all our affliction, so that we may be able to com-*
> *fort those who are in any affliction, with the comfort with*
> *which we ourselves are comforted by God.*
>
> —2 CORINTHIANS 1:3–4

Rick and I have spoken to numerous couples over the years, now, who have also had little ones go to heaven. As I stood on the doorstep of one grieving mother, readying myself for what I knew would be a heavy conversation, I heard the distinctive sound that had become my companion, the soft cooing song of our faithful mourning doves. And I knew that God was there not just for me but for her as well. God's comfort and love, instruction and teaching, discipline and direction are meant for all. He speaks to us in every conceivable way. His arm reaches out in defense of His own, not only with comfort and protection but also with confirmation. God is everywhere and in everything and has never once been silent as some presume. King David understood this and wrote in his Psalm,

> *Where shall I go from your Spirit? Or where shall I flee from your presence? If I ascend to heaven, you are there! If I make my bed in Sheol, you are there! If I take the wings of the morning and dwell in the uttermost parts of the sea, even there your hand shall lead me, and your right hand shall hold me. If I say, "Surely the darkness shall cover me, and the light about me be night," even the darkness is not dark to you; the night is bright as the day, for darkness is as light with you.*
>
> —Psalm 139:7–12

God is always at work in the world, even as He allows time for His plan and purpose to be played out in the earth. There is a gap of about 400 years between the Old and the New Testaments of our Bible, but rest assured that in those years, God's prophecy, given especially to His beloved Daniel, was happening just as He said it would. We are not alone in this world. God's voice shines through in every sunrise shouting light and life and new beginnings. The vastness of His character can be seen in the grace of a swan and the majesty of the great eagles. He sends us heavenly scents in the tea olive and gardenia and multiplies His praise with great lightnings and thunders. "He heals the brokenhearted and binds up their wounds" (Psalm 147:3). And He sends messages to His people "out of the mouth of babies and infants" (8:2).

One Sunday morning, Rick sat scribbling Bronner's name on his church bulletin, and as he looked at his son's name, he realized that there were seven letters in each one of his names, his first, middle, and last: William Bronner Burgess, 777. Rick handed me his scrawling, knowing I would see the meaning in it. He and I had often talked of Scripture numerics, noticing how God does seem to use certain numbers to emphasize a point. Seven is the number of completion, fullness, and perfection. It stands for the seven days of creation and is mentioned more than fifty times in the Book of Revelation, a book filled with sevens, for it reveals God's complete and perfect plan for the earth in its current state and ushers in a new heaven and a new earth where peace and perfection prevail. There are other significant numbers in the Bible. For example, three is the number of the Trinity, the number of God. Forty, as I have already mentioned, is sometimes used as a probationary period for God's people. But the number seven appears in Scripture more often than any other. That may be because God's Word itself is complete and perfect.

But the point was not missed, and we began to see other sevens in connection with Bronner. He is the seventh member of our family. The last full year of his life with us (for now) was 2007. His birthday is 5-27-2005. Add the five and the two before the seven and the five and the two after the seven, and again you get 777. He even has three sevens in his social security number, and I, his mother, was 37 when he went to heaven. Rick was 43. We believed that God was comforting us with all those many sevens, assuring us once again that our baby's life on earth is complete and perfect for now.

> *I praise you, for I am fearfully and wonderfully made. Wonderful are your works; my soul knows it very well. My frame was not hidden from you, when I was being made in secret, intricately woven in the depths of the earth. Your eyes saw my unformed substance; in your book were written, every one of them, the days that were formed for me, when as yet there were none of them.*
>
> —PSALM 139:14–16

> *Man who is born of a woman is few of days and full of trouble. He comes out like a flower and withers; he flees like a shadow and continues not . . . Since his days are determined, and the number of his months is with you, and you have appointed his limits that he cannot pass.*
>
> —JOB 14:1–5

On this both David and Job agree: that it is God who determines the number of our days. They are written in His book before we are even born. Our times are in His hands (Psalm 31:15). We cannot add a single hour to our span of life by worry (Matthew 6:27). Jesus Himself assured us of that. He also told us that not even a sparrow falls apart from the Father. "Fear not, therefore; you are of more value than many sparrows" (10:31).

I talked about the sevens when I was speaking at a women's conference at my home church, Shades Mountain Baptist, on August 16, 2008, one day after I had turned 38. I got a call that afternoon that the offering that had been collected for Bronner's Memorial Fund had totaled $7,777. (I think it was actually something like

$7,776.64, which of course rounds up to the next dollar.) I realized God had to have worked in the heart of every woman there in order to come up with that amount. No one knew what anyone else was giving, and no one was looking for that confirmation. There had been no expectation for that number, yet someone had even written a check for $1.23. I knew that the message God had given us about the sevens was spot on, for this was nothing short of a miracle. I saw it as confirmation from the Lord that we were on the right track. But when it happened again, I was absolutely astounded. The next year, also in August, I spoke at another women's event at Frazier Memorial United Methodist Church in Montgomery, Alabama. Betty Bussey, the wife of my husband's partner, Bill "Bubba" Bussey, also spoke that day. The sweet group of women who had coordinated the conference prepared refreshments for us afterward. We were all visiting together when the women's minister for their church came back with exciting news to tell me. She said happily, "We've collected more than $7,000 for Bronner's Memorial Fund today."

She didn't know there was anything special about that number, so I asked her, "Seven thousand and what, exactly?"

She said, "I don't know, but I can find out."

I told her what had happened at our church the year before, and she ran back to get an exact count. When she came back with the news, the young woman who had initially called me to speak at their women's event had to sit down. She had been at the Shades Mountain Baptist event and was impressed by the number of women who poured down the aisles to pray at the altar that day. She wanted the same thing for her church. She got it and so much more. Her name is Emily Roach, and she later blogged about it. She knew she had played a part in a miracle because the number her women's minister came back with was $7,774.77. Someone in the room added three dollars just to round it out, but we all knew we were witnessing the long reach of God's arm.

Of course, I was eager to tell Rick everything that had happened that day as soon as I got home. I knew that the women's ministry at Frazier supports Stella's Voice, which ministers to young girls in Moldova, a former Soviet country in Eastern Europe, who are turned out of orphanages at age 16 and become easy prey for sex trafficking. We had all but decided to give the entire $7,777.77 to the Montgomery-based ministry but had not mentioned this to anyone else. On Monday morning, the founder of the ministry's daughter, Melody, and some of her friends were standing outside the windows of *The Rick and Bubba Show* wearing Stella's Voice T-shirts. They had come to celebrate her birthday, even though they had not reserved "golden ticket" seats to come inside and watch their live radio broadcast. Rick noticed them standing outside listening through the speakers and invited them in. They talked about the ministry on the air that day, and a check was posted to the ministry for $7,777.77 from the Bronner Burgess Memorial Fund on August 25, 2009.

Remarkably, this isn't the end of the story. I was speaking at another church in Union Hill, Alabama, the next spring and told them about the sevens. I included the part about the check for $1.23 given at our church's event. There was so much more to my speech, but I included the story as an example of how God is very much alive and working among His people even today. I talked through weather sirens going off in the middle of my speech and through a woman passing out at the altar. I had driven through torrential rain to get there, and after leaving that night had to take an alternate route back home in order to avoid tornadoes. There was such bad weather forecast for that day in Alabama that no one would have blamed me if I had cancelled. But the Lord had me there if for no other reason than to meet a young woman who appeared to be in her early to midtwenties. She came up to me after the altar call while everyone else was still getting back to their seats and said to me through tears, "I thought you would think I was stupid for writing that amount, but it was all I had. It was me; I wrote that check for $1.23."

I grabbed her up so quickly and just held her for a few minutes while we both stood there crying in amazement at our very personal, very involved, and very active God. I told her, "God brought you here tonight so you could hear that story and know how special you are to God. He loves you so much!"

She answered, "Obviously!"

God is filled with good things. There is proof of His love everywhere. I never asked for God to do these things. He just did them. I wasn't looking for a miracle. I wasn't looking for confirmation. I was just looking for God. I found Him, and I have found that His great love is better than anything. I love the Lord more than I love anything. I hope you can see that in these lines. He is my all in all, and I can't find enough praise in my lungs to do Him any justice at all. He is magnificent. He is holy. He is wonderful. There is no one and no thing like Him. To know Him defies description. He is beyond measure. He is beyond wise.

There is cunning and cruelty in Satan. His wisdom is sneaky and sly, slithering around on the ground looking for a chance to strike. But God's wisdom is born in love. The best and wisest grandfather on earth could never compare to Him, for He is incomparable. His love is so vast, the Bible tells us, that it never ends. I have been taken up and wrapped up and held in that love. I have been doted over and fretted upon like a rare jewel by my God. I have felt it. I have felt His pleasure and love for me. And, I pray to my God today that this little offering here, this token of my love and gratitude, is pleasing in His sight. *Take it, my Lord and my Love, and do with it what You will. Amen.*

God is called "the Father of mercies and God of all comfort" in 2 Corinthians 1:3. He is called the God of endurance and encouragement in Romans 15:5. He is everything we need to make it through any bad thing this world has for us, and we will need Him. We need His mercy, comfort, and encouragement in order to endure. The testing and trying by fire is hard. It hurts, and that's OK. God expects us to grieve. When James tells us to "count it all joy" (James 1:2) when we meet trials of various kinds, he doesn't mean that the trial itself will be joyful. The joy is for what it will produce in us and in others, not the pain itself. It's OK to cry and to be mournful. There is a time for weeping. In fact, James tells us that we should mourn especially over our own sinful selves.

> *"God opposes the proud, but gives grace to the humble." Submit yourselves therefore to God. Resist the devil, and he will flee from you. Draw near to God, and he will draw near to you. Cleanse your hands, you sinners, and purify your hearts, you double-minded. Be wretched and mourn and weep. Let your laughter be turned to mourning and your joy to gloom. Humble yourselves before the Lord, and he will exalt you.*
>
> —JAMES 4:6–10

And when Paul tells us to "rejoice" in Philippians 4, he doesn't say to rejoice in just anything, but to rejoice "in the Lord" (v. 4). We are not to rejoice in evil or injustice or wrongdoing, but we are to rejoice *in the Lord*. We rejoice in the fact that no matter how bad the situation is, He's not only there with us through it all but He also provides hope that it won't always be like this. We rejoice that it will be OK in the end, and that no matter what, we have a very bright future with Him. Press on, soldier. Keep going. The night is almost over. The day is close at hand.

God *is* love, and everything He does is out of His great love for us. People always want to know, "If God is good then why does He allow bad things?" I have learned that He does it out of love. He doesn't want us to be in love with this fallen world. He wants us to be in love with Him. Because He is greater than anything this world has to offer. God is love, but He is also just. And His holiness requires a reckoning for sin. But even in this, He provides a way of love. "Greater love has no one than this, that someone lay down his life for his friends" (John 15:13). Jesus did just that. He laid down his life for you and for me, to be the propitiation for sin so "that whoever believes in him should not perish but have eternal life" (John 3:16). "In this world," in this one, we "will have trouble. But take heart!" He has "overcome the world" (16:33 NIV). And because He has overcome the world, so can we. We can walk in the way of love (Ephesians 5:2).

In 1 Corinthians 13:1–3, the Apostle Paul says:

> *If I speak in the tongues of men and of angels, but have not love, I am a noisy gong or a clanging cymbal. And if I have prophetic powers, and understand all mysteries and all knowledge, and if I have all faith, so as to remove mountains, but have not love, I am nothing. If I give away all I have, and if I deliver up my body to be burned, but have not love, I gain nothing.*

If God is love, then we can put *God* in place of the word *love* here and understand that Paul means that without God, it's all pointless. Anything he ever did apart from Jesus Christ, the Lord, gained him nothing. People place their faith in a lot of things, but unless it's God, the triune Father, Son, and Holy Spirit, we gain nothing.

"So now faith, hope, and love abide, these three; but the greatest of these is love" (1 Corinthians 13:13).

Love is the greatest of these because love came first. If not for our sin, we wouldn't have to hope, we wouldn't have to have faith because we wouldn't be separated from God.

"But thanks be to God, who gives us the victory through our Lord Jesus Christ" (15:57).

> *For I am sure that neither death nor life, nor angels nor rulers, nor things present nor things to come, nor powers, nor height nor depth, nor anything else in all creation, will be able to separate us from the love of God in Christ Jesus our Lord.*
>
> —Romans 8:38–39

I ask you today, is there anything greater than the love of God? Is there anything more pure and holy? Is there anything better?

Why would we choose anything else?

Love God. Serve Him only.

And, why not?

God is patient and kind. He doesn't envy or boast. He isn't arrogant or rude. He doesn't insist on His own way. He isn't irritable or resentful. He doesn't rejoice at wrongdoing but rejoices with the truth. God bears all things, believes all things, hopes all things, endures all things . . . for you (1 Corinthians 13:4–7).

We, like Jesus, are to endure suffering while fixing our eyes and hearts on the joy that is set before us. The hallelujahs are coming. Jesus is coming. Heaven is coming.

All of it is for you and for me, and if He is willing to make so much of us, then we should be willing to make that much more of Him.

"What is man, that you make so much of him, and that you set your heart on him, visit him every morning and test him every moment?" (Job 7:17–18).

Job was a man tested by God with great tribulation and bitter distress, and in the midst of it all Job cries out for a Redeemer such as Christ to save him:

> *For I know that my Redeemer lives, and at the last he will stand upon the earth. And after my skin has been thus destroyed, yet in my flesh I shall see God, whom I shall see for myself, and my eyes shall behold, and not another. My heart faints within me!*
>
> —JOB 19:25–27

Job was brought forward to the Cross of Christ long, long ago. His suffering, and ours, is meant to identify us with our suffering Savior.

"For to this you have been called, because Christ also suffered for you, leaving you an example, so that you might follow in his steps" (1 Peter 2:21).

"Whoever loves his life loses it, and whoever hates his life in this world will keep it for eternal life. If anyone serves me, he must follow me; and where I am, there will my servant be also" (John 12:25–26).

Follow Him to the Cross, and you will also follow Him to glory. C. S. Lewis states it this way, "The cross comes before the crown." The Apostle Paul put it like this,

> *The Spirit himself bears witness with our spirit that we are children of God, and if children, then heirs — heirs of*

God and fellow heirs with Christ, provided we suffer with him in order that we may also be glorified with him.

—ROMANS 8:16–17

That, my friends, is a conditional statement. If we are His, we *will* suffer with Him. And when that fiery trial comes upon us to test us, we are to submit to it as "a good soldier of Christ Jesus" (2 Timothy 2:3). "It is for discipline that you have to endure" (Hebrews 12:7). Not discipline in the sense of punishment, but discipline as in training. "Do you not know that in a race all the runners run, but only one receives the prize? So run that you may obtain it" (1 Corinthians 9:24).

God beseeches us,

Beloved, do not be surprised at the fiery trial when it comes upon you to test you, as though something strange were happening to you. But rejoice insofar as you share Christ's sufferings, that you may also rejoice and be glad when his glory is revealed.

—1 PETER 4:12–13

We have no idea what kind of fiery trial we might be brought unto, for it is the Lord who sanctifies. But my prayer is this, that the children of God come out better for it. Never let go of the One who pulled you up out of darkness in the first place. And when it hurts the most, endure, for "by your endurance, you will gain your lives" (Luke 21:19).

May you be strengthened with all power, according to his glorious might, for all endurance and patience with joy,

giving thanks to the Father, who has qualified you to share
in the inheritance of the saints in light.

—COLOSSIANS 1:11–12

Suffering produces in us endurance and character and hope (Romans 5:3–4). It steadies us in our faith and deepens its roots in order that we may be able to weather any storm. It makes us reach forward to greater things than we can see right now but that we know for sure not only exist, but will be ours at the last.

Humble yourselves, therefore, under the mighty hand of
God so that at the proper time he may exalt you, casting
all your anxieties on him, because he cares for you. Be
sober-minded; be watchful. Your adversary the devil
prowls around like a roaring lion, seeking someone to
devour. Resist him, firm in your faith, knowing that the
same kinds of suffering are being experienced by your
brotherhood throughout the world. And after you have
suffered a little while, the God of all grace, who has called
you to his eternal glory in Christ, will himself restore,
confirm, strengthen, and establish you.

—1 PETER 5:6–10

God, Himself, will "restore, confirm, strengthen, and establish you."

We, like Jesus, are to endure suffering while fixing our eyes and hearts on the joy that is set before us. The hallelujahs are coming. Jesus is coming. Heaven is coming. But for now, we work out our salvation with fear and trembling knowing that the prize is yet to come.

We endure now for the glory that is to come later.

> *So then, brothers, we are debtors, not to the flesh, to live according to the flesh. For if you live according to the flesh you will die, but if by the Spirit you put to death the deeds of the body, you will live. For all who are led by the Spirit of God are sons of God. For you did not receive the spirit of slavery to fall back into fear, but you have received the Spirit of adoption as sons, by whom we cry, "Abba! Father!"*
>
> —ROMANS 8:12–15

We must deem Him worthy of our suffering and trust that all of it is for the high calling of Christ. Submit to the crucifixion, the pruning, and grow to bear ever more fruit as each year brings us closer and closer to glory.

"Let those who suffer according to God's will entrust their souls to a faithful Creator while doing good" (1 Peter 4:19).

It's not easy to bear these things. Crucifixion hurts. It crushes to the uttermost. That is exactly why God is there for us in the fire. The king was astonished, the Bible says, and asked, "Did we not cast three men bound into the fire?" (Daniel 3:24). "But I see four men unbound, walking in the midst of the fire, and they are not hurt; and the appearance of the fourth is like a son of the gods" (v. 25).

I *know* that it was Jesus in that fiery furnace with Shadrach, Meshach, and Abednego, for He has certainly been in mine with me. And like the great king of Babylon, I have been humbled under His hand.

Who teaches like the Lord? No one is certainly the answer.

It has been almost ten years now since that September day in 2004 when I prayed for God to set me on a course to crucify the sin in my life in accordance with Galatians 5:24, "Those who belong to Christ Jesus have crucified the flesh with its passions and desires" (NIV).

God's answer to my prayer was Bronner.

On New Year's Day morning 2009, as we were about to embark on a journey to Israel to be there for the first anniversary of Bronner's heaven-going, I sat outside on the front porch of our little farmhouse in Jemison, wrapped in a blanket that had been knitted and prayed over for me by some sweet women from our church, and God brought me to this verse:

> *Since therefore Christ suffered in the flesh, arm yourselves*
> *with the same way of thinking, for whoever has suffered*
> *in the flesh has ceased from sin, so as to live for the rest of*
> *the time in the flesh no longer for human passions but for*
> *the will of God.*
>
> —1 PETER 4:1–2

Today as I am finishing this chapter in the book of my life, I stand crucified with Christ and yet do I live. "I have been crucified with Christ. It is no longer I who live, but Christ who lives in me. And the life I now live in the flesh I live by faith in the Son of God, who loved me and gave himself for me" (Galatians 2:20).

This is my prayer:

Oh blessed Father, let this great sanctification be complete, not that I may leave this life and enter into heaven but that I may be a true example for the believers and empirical evidence of Your power, glory, majesty, and truth. I asked You to crucify the sin in my life on September 27, 2004. You have done what I asked. You have pruned and cultivated this little tree of Yours and made it to grow with precious fruit to feed the people with.

I can see Your hand. I see Your purpose. I see how perfect it really was, and I stand back amazed. Who teaches like the Lord? No one is certainly the answer. Your ways are undeniably higher than ours, for no person alive could have guessed that the thing that would purify me more than anything would be to take away my beautiful blessing Bronner at the most fun and fantastic age of all, two and a half. Little baby boys running around with such vitality, curiosity, laughter, and beauty are such a joy to every mother's heart, but I cannot imagine anyone loving and adoring and cherishing one more than I did Bronner.

You are very unexpected, Lord. And I know You did not find pleasure in my pain, but You knew that my tears would wash my soul of all its worldliness, pride, and self-reliance. And now I know that You are better than anything, a great God and Savior who sanctifies my soul and makes me fit for the splendor of Your holy kingdom. I pray I will continue in holiness, fervor, adoration, and amazement of You, Your ways, Your sovereignty, Your wisdom and perfection, Your grace, mercy, and love. I know that everything I have been through is because of Your great love for me, that You were perfecting me, washing me, teaching me for my own good and for Your glory, and that is the very thing I want to do: glorify You!

So thank You, dear Father, dear Savior and Friend, Holy Spirit, all three, You, oh God, have taught me well. And I will ever praise You for it.

In Jesus' name, amen.

Thursday, August 14, 2014

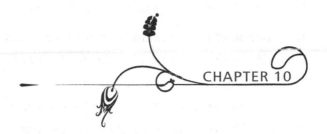

THE LIVING WILL LAY IT TO HEART

The Bible says that the day of death is better than the day of birth.
Really?

"A good name is better than precious ointment, and the day of death than the day of birth" (Ecclesiastes 7:1).

The day of death, better than the day of birth . . .

I believe this. I believe every word written in the Bible to be true, that they are the very words of God, His revelation of Himself to man, that they were recorded by holy men of old but were "breathed out" by God and are "profitable for teaching, for reproof, for correction, and for training in righteousness" (2 Timothy 3:16).

We are not left in the dark as to who God is, why we are here, how sin and death entered our world, nor what God's plan is for its redemption. Without some explanation, who could stand? But we are not left without answers, and we are not left alone. And this is a lesson in righteousness taught by God.

The day of death *is* better than the day of birth.

But I remember both in the life of my son. I remember the day he was born and how happy I was. I remember holding him close to me and feeling the warmth of a newborn baby cradled in my arms. I remember the excitement and joy that filled the room, Rick's smile, wide-eyed boys filled with wonder, eager to hold him, too. It was a day filled with inexplicable beauty.

The day of Bronner's earthly death was something altogether different. There was certainly awe, not of death, but of God. There was certainly mystery, but it wasn't the light and airy kind that makes you feel all fuzzy inside like I had felt at the birth of my baby. It was more of the dark and foreboding kind that gives way to dread and leads to fear. It was the difference in clouds and sunshine, and not those fluffy white ones either. I'm talking about the ominous, threatening ones.

Before that day, I only knew one side of God, the forgiving, kind, loving one. But on the day Bronner went to heaven, I began to see God in a different light . . . I saw Him as King above all things, beyond understanding, beyond my reach or grasp.

So I must look beyond myself, beyond my own experience, beyond the here and now, to God. I must look to God to see how the day of Bronner's death, despite all appearances, was better than the day of his birth.

When Bronner was born into heaven, he was born into sparkling light brighter than the most beautiful summer day, a place where there is no decay or death of any kind. You would never see an animal lying in the road hit by oncoming traffic, and you would certainly never see vultures or crows picking at it. But this is a very common occurrence where I live in Indian Springs, Alabama. I think we're numb to that kind of thing because that's all we know. I like to put flowers on my table. Once, when they were fading, Brody said to me, "I hate when flowers die." Where Bronner lives, they don't. Here they last such a short time.

The cycle of life and death flows in and out and up and down and all around. In the woods at our farm, there are fallen trees everywhere. Some fell a while back when all the tornadoes came through our state. I say "all" because there was a day in April a few years ago that sent more than 60 tornadoes through Alabama in one day. There was incredible devastation and loss of life. But most of the fallen trees lying on the floor of the woods at our farm just fell. Maybe it was some kind of bug that killed it. Or maybe it was lightning. Maybe it was just old. So many things can make a tree fall. But where Bronner is, they don't. There is only life. The trees grow big and strong, and he can climb up in them and never fear falling. He's safe. He doesn't skin his knee or bruise or break an arm like Brody did once. And the people . . . I can't even imagine the cool people he gets to meet and see.

I've thought about birthday parties with Noah himself telling the story of the ark and the flood and animal rides, but in heaven the animal rides aren't just ponies or camels or something you would normally think of riding. I'm thinking lions and giraffes. But the best part is God Himself. Here we're separated from Him. We can't look at Him. But Bronner sees God every day. He sees both Father and Son, and he's not afraid. He doesn't have to be. He's safe and happy and loved.

On the day Bronner was born to me, he was born into sin, danger, and darkness. Where he had been born into my arms, he now rests in God's . . . well, for a moment or two before he has to get down to run some more. I know Bronner. God, the Father, and Jesus, the Son, are beyond comprehension. To be there with God is something I can't describe. I've never been, but I can imagine, and I know from what is written that Bronner isn't disappointed with his new home and his Father and Friend and Savior. God doesn't disappoint. How could He? He's perfect!

Ecclesiastes 7:2 continues, "It is better to go to the house of mourning than to go to the house of feasting, for this is the end of all mankind, and the living will lay it to heart."

The living will lay it to heart.

What seems to be isn't always what it really is. We can clearly see that Bronner's reality is better in heaven than my reality here on earth. That's easy. But God doesn't mean it for my harm either. He means it for good, not just Bronner's good, but mine, too. I, the living, would lay it to heart. What does it all mean?

Before that day, I only knew one side of God, the forgiving, kind, loving one. But on the day Bronner went to heaven, I began to see God in a different light. I saw His power, authority, might, majesty, justice, integrity, omnipotence . . . I could go on and on. I saw Him as King above all things, beyond understanding, beyond my reach or grasp. I saw Him as greater, higher, bigger than I had ever seen Him before. None of this was bad, just different, deeper.

I had to know this side of God, too. I had to know why. It made me search it all out, search Him out. I had never thought that much about heaven before, but now I wanted to know everything. And I hadn't even noticed all the verses upon verses and passages upon passages of Scripture that talk about suffering. I hadn't needed to. I needed them now, and they were there.

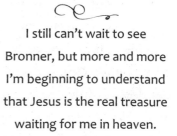

I still can't wait to see Bronner, but more and more I'm beginning to understand that Jesus is the real treasure waiting for me in heaven.

In what was most likely Paul's last letter before he was martyred, 2 Timothy, we are instructed again and again to "share in suffering for the gospel" (1:8). "Share in suffering as a good soldier of Christ Jesus" (2:3). And "if we endure, we will also reign with him" (2:12). "Endure suffering, do the work of an evangelist, fulfill your ministry" (4:5).

At the end of his life, writing from a prison cell, the Apostle Paul knew about suffering for the Lord. He had been beaten, run out of town, stoned, imprisoned, shipwrecked, snake-bitten, blinded. He had traveled and preached and worked with all the zeal and commitment and passion his earthly tent could muster. He did all he was commanded to do, and he did it with joy, joy in knowing that he was faithful to God. And at the end of it all, he was able to say:

> *I have fought the good fight, I have finished the race, I have kept the faith. Henceforth there is laid up for me the crown of righteousness, which the Lord, the righteous judge, will award to me on that Day, and not only to me but also to all who have loved his appearing.*
>
> —2 TIMOTHY 4:7–8

He was looking to the crown, to God, to heaven, to the glory he knew would be waiting for him. He wanted eternity, but not prematurely. He had told the Philippians from a different prison at an earlier time that he was eager to see them again, but whether that was to be or not to be was all up to God. He told them that he just wanted to honor Christ, whether by life or by death. Either way. He said, "For to me to live is Christ, and to die is gain. If I am to live in the flesh, that means fruitful labor for me" (Philippians 1:21–22). But, "My desire is to depart and be with Christ, for that is far better. But to remain in the flesh is more necessary on your account. Convinced of this, I know that I will remain and continue with you all, for your progress and joy in the faith" (vv. 23–25).

Paul had been given the special privilege of seeing heaven (2 Corinthians 12:2–7). He'd been there. He didn't know if it were in his body or out of his body. He couldn't tell, but he knew it was "far better" than here, and he did want to go there. But for the sake

That is why Bronner went to heaven. Sin separated me from him, and sin separated me from God. But one day there will be a feast to celebrate the fact that we will never be apart again.

of the gospel, he remained on earth. God had work for him to do, and he did it. When he was finished with the work God had called him to, he departed just as so many others had.

In Acts 12, we see James, the brother of John, killed by Herod Agrippa; but in the very same chapter, Peter is miraculously rescued by an angel. We're all called to something, and that something is different for everyone else. James was called to die, but God had more work for Peter to do on earth before he would be martyred as well. The thing that really stands out to me from Acts 12 is what the angel says to Peter. He says three things: (1) "Get up quickly" (v. 7). (2) "Dress yourself and put on your sandals" (v. 8). (3) "Wrap your cloak around you and follow me" (v. 8). This stands in direct contrast to what God said to Moses in the Old Testament. He said from the burning bush, "Do not come near; take your sandals off your feet, for the place on which you are standing is holy ground" (Exodus 3:5). Moses was about to learn who God is, and in turn, he would teach others. That's what the Old Testament is about, learning who God is and what His standards are.

But the New Testament is about action. If you already know God, get up, put your working boots on, and get to work. Peter was the epitome of this. He was the man of action. We have the benefit of both. We can know who God is, *and* we can dress ourselves for action. But the work of God is different for each one. God called me to write this book. I don't think I could have ever felt complete until this work was done. I don't know what the next step is for me. I just know that I was called to write a book. Bronner's work was different. Whether by death or by life, we honor God. Was Peter more loved than James? Highly unlikely. But Peter lived and James died. God chooses one for one work and another for another work. One is not better or worse, but it is all to further the kingdom of God. The fact that these early Christians were so willing to give up their lives for the faith caused quite a stir. People stood up and took notice. Their thinking must have gone something like this: "If they're willing to die for it, they must really believe. I wonder if there's something to it." We've all heard that the church was built on the blood of the martyrs. Maybe. I do know one thing: that not one person died who wasn't supposed to die, and not one person lived who wasn't supposed to live because God is sovereign. He is in control. Not even a sparrow falls apart from the Lord (Matthew 10:29).

If because of Bronner's earthly death, one person comes to know the Lord, he has borne fruit for God. He has been a good soldier of Christ Jesus. And we know there have been many. This is good and pleasing to the Lord. This is His will, and I hope Bronner will continue to bear fruit for the Lord as long as there is fruit to be born in this earth. I pray this book will be a part of that and that wherever Bronner is remembered, God will be exalted, for all of this has been for the glory of God and His kingdom.

Better is the end of a thing than its beginning, and the patient in spirit is better than the proud in spirit. Be not quick in your spirit to become angry, for anger lodges in the heart of fools. Say not, "Why were the former days better than these?" For it is not from wisdom that you ask this. Wisdom is good with an inheritance, an advantage to those who see the sun. For the protection of wisdom is like the protection of money, and the advantage of knowledge is that wisdom preserves the life of him who has it. Consider the work of God: who can make straight what he has made crooked? In the day of prosperity be joyful, and in the day of adversity consider: God has made the one as well as the other, so that man may not find out anything that will be after him.

—ECCLESIASTES 7:8–14

In the beginning, I did look back and long for the days when all the children were around me. I'm sure many parents do this even as their kids grow up and go off to college and get married and start their own families. Change is hard, and it takes time to get used to. I had been used to being with Bronner all the time, and I missed him desperately. Everything changed in an instant, and I didn't like it. My world had been turned upside down, and I wanted it turned right side up. What I really wanted more than anything else was Bronner. He was the object of my desire. I wanted heaven so I could be with Bronner. But over time, in all of my seeking, there's been a shift. I believe it to be the right one. I still can't wait to see Bronner, but more and more I'm beginning to understand that Jesus is the real treasure waiting for me in heaven. My inheritance is Jesus—imperishable, undefiled, and unfading, kept in heaven for me.

I have learned that Jesus isn't just a means to an end. He is the end. He is the Alpha and the Omega, the beginning and the end, the Almighty. Yes, He holds the keys to everything else we desire, everything we hope for, eternal life, heaven, a glorious reunion with those we love. But He tells us to "seek first the kingdom of God and his righteousness, and all these things will be added to you" (Matthew 6:33).

Seek Him first. Know Him first.

First and foremost . . . Jesus.

David knew this well. He wrote about it and sang about it all the time. God first, last, and everything in between, the object of my desire.

Listen to his words from the Psalms:

> As a deer pants for flowing streams, so pants my soul for you, O God. My soul thirsts for God, for the living God. When shall I come and appear before God?
>
> —PSALM 42:1–2, AUTHOR'S EMPHASIS

> Cast me not away from your presence, and take not your Holy Spirit from me.
>
> —51:11

> O my God, be not far from me!
>
> —38:21

> The LORD is my shepherd; I shall not want . . . I shall dwell in the house of the LORD forever.
>
> —23:1, 6

Can't you hear him saying, "That's where I want to be, in His house, in His presence?"

> But for you, O LORD, do I wait; it is you, O Lord my God, who will answer.
>
> —PSALM 38:15

> For God alone my soul waits in silence; from him comes my salvation. He alone is my rock and my salvation, my fortress; I shall not be greatly shaken.
>
> —62:1–2, AUTHOR'S EMPHASIS

But I trust in you, O LORD; I say, "You are my God." My times are in your hand.

—31:14–15

Bless the LORD, O my soul, and all that is within me, bless his holy name! Bless the LORD, O my soul, and forget not all his benefits, who forgives all your iniquity, who heals all your diseases, who redeems your life from the pit, who crowns you with steadfast love and mercy, who satisfies you with good so that your youth is renewed like the eagle's.

—103:1–5

Great is the LORD, and greatly to be praised.

—145:3

Praise the LORD!

—148:1; 149:1; 150:1

So many people place their hopes and their desires in other people, in things, in positions, power, glory for themselves.

But not David.

He loved people. He had a great kinship and oneness of spirit with Jonathan, his friend. He was a man and loved women. He wanted another man's wife, as we know, and this was his great sin. We all have great sins, but do we have great love, great repentance, the desire to please God, to do nothing that would jeopardize the relationship we have with Him, and when we do, to be completely broken by it, as David was?

David loved the Lord above all things and all people. He messed up, yeah. We all do. But he repented of his sin and pleaded with the Lord for mercy.

THE LIVING WILL LAY IT TO HEART

Why?

Because he didn't want to be separated from God. God was and is his all in all.

Paul said in Romans 8:18, "For I consider that the sufferings of this present time are not worth comparing with the glory that is to be revealed to us."

Not worth comparing?

It can get a little rough down here, God.

But He says, "Hold on. Trust me. Wait on Me. It's all going to be worth it. Don't worry. Don't fret. I am making all things new."

"For in this hope we were saved. Now hope that is seen is not hope. For who hopes for what he sees? But if we hope for what we do not see, we wait for it with patience" (vv. 24–25).

What we hope for is coming.

Everything we desire. All that we could ever hope for or imagine—"No eye has seen, nor ear heard, nor the heart of man imagined, what God has prepared for those who love him" (1 Corinthians 2:9).

But "these things God has revealed to us through the Spirit," Paul said, "for the Spirit searches everything, even the depths of God" (v. 10).

It's the Holy Spirit within me who confirms everything I believe and makes me sure.

I have the full assurance of hope that through my faith and patience, I will inherit the promises. I will inherit Jesus. And Bronner comes with Him. Bronner is there. He is my Bronner. But I have learned that my Jesus is first . . . first and foremost, the object of my desire.

"This hope we have as an anchor of the soul, both sure and steadfast, and which enters the Presence behind the veil, where the forerunner has

entered for us, even Jesus, having become High Priest forever" (Hebrews 6:19–20 NKJV).

I *can* say with Job, "Though he slay me, I will hope in him" (Job 13:15). Because I know, I know, that He is greater than death.

> *He has made my teeth grind on gravel, and made me cower in ashes; my soul is bereft of peace; I have forgotten what happiness is; so I say, "My endurance has perished; so has my hope from the LORD." Remember my affliction and my wanderings, the wormwood and the gall! My soul continually remembers it and is bowed down within me. But this I call to mind, and therefore I have hope: The steadfast love of the LORD never ceases; his mercies never come to an end; they are new every morning; great is your faithfulness. "The LORD is my portion," says my soul, "therefore I will hope in him."*
>
> —LAMENTATIONS 3:16–24

The *Lord* is my portion, says my soul, therefore I will hope in Him.

In *Him*.

Let the storms rage. We say to them, "We are founded on the *Rock*."

"And the rain fell, and the floods came, and the winds blew and beat on that house, but it did not fall, because it had been founded on the rock" (Matthew 7:25).

Welcome it.

"For the moment all discipline seems painful rather than pleasant, but later it yields the peaceful fruit of righteousness to those who have been trained by it" (Hebrews 12:11).

Understanding is imperative. I wanted to know why. I wanted to know where Bronner is and what he might be doing. I wanted to know everything I could about this whole situation. I thought you might be wondering, too. That is why I wanted to share what I have found. If we walk around in the dark wondering why, why we are here, why we suffer, what is it all for . . . then I don't believe we can catch the fever of the fire of God that is to make us better. It's all about God creating for Himself a people who understand His power and appreciate His majesty so that we may be one with Him and share in His glory and the beauty that is coming with Him. Yes, we will suffer with Him, but the pain of today brings the peace and purpose of tomorrow. God doesn't allow our suffering to hurt us but to help us so that we will look not to the things of the world as the object of our desire but instead place our hopes on high, on Him. Because He is good. He loves us. He loves us enough to rip our hearts right out of this world and place them in heaven, where He is, sitting at the right hand of God.

Do you understand?

It is all for good. Everything. And at the last, we will have seen His glory, His omnipotence, His grace, His good, His love, His trustworthiness, and we *will know* that it has all been worth it.

That is why Bronner went to heaven. Sin separated me from him, and sin separated me from God. But one day there will be a feast to celebrate the fact that we will never be apart again. That is what I am longing for. That is what I am living for. I wait with eager expectation upon that Day, but in the meantime, I will be about His business. I will be about His business. Wherever He leads, I *will* follow.

"My sheep hear my voice, and I know them, and they follow me" (John 10:27).

Be His, dear reader. Enter His gates with thanksgiving. Devote your life to Him, and trust His leading. He is the Good Shepherd who laid down His life for the sheep. He will never leave you nor

Find your way to God and then be a road map for others to find Him as well.

forsake you. He will lift you up out of the deep waters and become a refreshing spring to your soul. Let Him. Let Him be Father and Friend and Redeemer. He brings beauty from ashes and gardens out of deserts. He is able. And when your own heart condemns you, know that He is greater than your heart. Ask and you will be given life everlasting. Seek and you will see a Savior filled with good things. Follow and find fellowship with God Himself and with a family of believers who will come along beside you to cheer you on your way. It's real. It's really real, the love, the companionship, the everything. God is real. There's so much evidence, so have faith, faith in the one true God who is Father, Son, and Holy Spirit. And then allow Him to grow you for good, yours, His, and for the many people who already have fellowship with Him and also for those who don't. As Christians, we are called to encourage one another, love one another, and build each other up through prayer and fellowship and teaching, but we are also called to witness to the lost. There are so many out there searching. God has set eternity in our hearts so that we will look for Him. Find your way to God and then be a road map for others to find Him as well.

God bless you in your journey and know that I am praying for you. Thank you for allowing me into your life for this moment. I hope you have been challenged and changed for good.

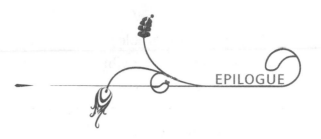

EPILOGUE

I wrote this book over the course of five years, not all at once, but in breaks and starts and in spurts. I felt God calling me to write it very early on but realized my life would have to change in order to do so. I was doing a lot of speaking in that first year that Bronner went to heaven. And I had not given up one thing that I had been involved in before. I still taught Sunday School and attended Community Bible Study. I was even still involved in the Parent Teacher Fellowship at my children's school. The first two chapters were written very quickly during that time of raw grief and memories. I then put the book aside until a time when I could fully devote myself to it. I gave up teaching for a while. I stopped working with the Parent Teacher Fellowship at my kids' school. I even gave up Community Bible Study and speaking for a time. But I found that a wife and mother can never fully devote herself to anything that doesn't include her husband and children. So my time was still divided. This was God's will. He wanted it to be a journey. I still had to work through so much. Time and eternity had to come into focus. There was a lot of grieving still to do and questions to be answered. If I had completed the book in 2009, when I started it, it wouldn't be the book it is today. Time is what makes the finest of wines and the best of cheeses, so they say. And time is what I needed, but I didn't see that until the end of the matter.

At first, I was desperate to complete the book. I felt that time was of the essence, and I became anxious about it. But the more anxious

I became, the less I was able to write. And those first two chapters needed work, I thought. I edited and reedited those two chapters until I had three different versions of them. I was in a quandary. I didn't know what else to do but to give them to Rick and ask him. But he loved them, all of them. "So what do I do?"

"Well, that's got to be in there," Rick said, "And that. There are parts of all of them that are good. Combine them."

So that's what I did. It took forever to get those first two chapters right, and by that time everything had changed. Bronner would have already finished four-year-old kindergarten. Cynthia wasn't working for me anymore. Nothing was the same, not even my perspective. The answer? Date it. It's that simple. Sigh. But I wondered if I was just subconsciously afraid to move on to chapter 3. Chapter 3 hung over me like a plague. I didn't want to go there. Who on earth would? What I was writing about seemed like a crucifixion, one I had never signed up for, but the writing about it? I signed up for that. I was willingly submitting to a second crucifixion. And it hurt. It hurt so badly. I could barely read through what had already been written without finding myself in a heap on the floor, wailing uncontrollably and barely able to get my breath.

Those chapters were written at the farm in complete solitude. They needed to be. Chapter 4 was a gift to Rick for his birthday one year. He loved it. He's been cheering me on about this book for so long. He loves my writing. He has never once disliked something I've written. He's so proud of me. It's sweet. But more than that, He could see that God wanted this thing done, that it was God's will for me. He would remind me time and again that I had told him that I believed this was my life's purpose and would be, along with my children, my greatest contribution to the world.

Chapter 5 was almost as difficult for me to write as the third chapter. Maybe it was because I couldn't feel good about saying anything that could be misrepresented or mistaken for criticism of my church. I love my church. It is a refreshing spring of water to my soul that fills me up each Sunday morning, so much so that I live in the glow of its worshipful trough all week long until I can drink again at its waters. My church family rallied around me in my grief. It seemed every sermon and every song sung for months, and maybe even years, had me in mind. Michael Adler, our minister of music, is the closest and best of friends, and our senior pastor, Danny Wood, couldn't help but be changed by what he saw and has seen beginning on the night Bronner went to heaven and beyond. He has certainly been a great part of this story.

One year and one month after Bronner went to heaven, our church family had another great tragedy and had to work through it all again. We've grown together through much grief and despair, hurt, pain, betrayal, disappointments, one right after the other. But we've also experienced great strides in bringing the gospel around the world. I, personally, have been to Africa twice, India, and Israel on missions trips. Rick, Brooks, and Brody have also been to Nicaragua. Brandi's been to Mexico on mission. And I hope there are many other places we'll go in time, or maybe just back to the same places again and again. Our congregation has been all around the world not only for short-term missions trips, but many have also taken up the call to full-time missions work to all parts of our globe. Our giving is beyond comparison, consistently going above and beyond most churches our size.

The message of my chapter 5 on the lukewarm condition of the church wasn't for my church alone but for the church at large, all of us together, including myself. It was about revival, works and worship together, deepening our understanding of God, coming face to face with His power and majesty and glory. And even if the desire was there, the fire had not been lit. We were and are a refreshing spring, but now the fire also burns brightly within us. This is precisely the way revival of the church comes, one member at a time.

So I kept rewriting that first part over and over again, but I always came back to the original version. It took me a long time to finish chapter 5. It felt like Wednesday; if I could just get over this hump, the weekend would be right around the corner. But God taught me so much through that chapter. As I finished writing it and read back through it, I gasped. I couldn't believe what I was just realizing. It was another one of those "wow" moments you only get once in a while. To see what I mean, I want you read through this passage on the Laodicean church from Revelation again, and then I'll explain.

> And to the angel of the church in Laodicea write: "The words of the Amen, the faithful and true witness, the beginning of God's creation. I know your works: you are neither cold nor hot. Would that you were either cold or hot! So, because you are lukewarm, and neither hot nor cold, I will spit you out of my mouth. For you say, I am rich, I have prospered, and I need nothing, not realizing that you are wretched, pitiable, poor, blind, and naked. I counsel you to buy from me gold refined by fire, so that you may be rich, and white garments so that you may clothe yourself and the shame of your nakedness may not be seen, and salve to anoint your eyes, so that you may see. Those whom I love, I reprove and discipline, so be zealous and repent. Behold, I stand at the door and knock. If anyone hears my voice and opens the door, I will come in to him and eat with him, and he with me. The one who conquers, I will grant him to sit with me on my

throne, as I also conquered and sat down with my Father
on his throne. He who has an ear, let him hear what the
Spirit says to the churches.

—REVELATION 3:14–22, AUTHOR'S EMPHASIS

If God used that passage of Scripture to begin the process of revival in me in 2007, He is still using it today. As I read back through everything that God prompted me to write, for this has been a work of the Holy Spirit from beginning to end, I began to marvel at what God has done. Indeed, it didn't really strike me until I finished that chapter, that when I opened the door for revival in my own spirit and repented of the sin of my own lukewarm condition, God not only set my soul ablaze with the fire of His own Spirit, He allowed Satan to begin kindling the fire for me to be cast into, which God would use to refine my walk, open my eyes to see the eternal, and clothe me in His holiness and truth. I had read the counsel Jesus gave to the Laodicean church, but I didn't quite understand it until it was actually down on paper in my own story. God's Spirit helped me to write the words, and even I stand back amazed at God's revealed truth. When I can see the evidence of Scripture being worked out in my own life, God's existence is proved that much more. His presence with me makes me stand in awe of Him ever more.

The rest of the book flowed out pretty easily after that. I believe chapter 5 is the message, the central truth behind it all. It's the chapter that means to set the soul ablaze for God's holiness and truth, even mine. God revealed all of it, the big picture, over the process of time. And only after the work was complete could I look back and see what all He had done. So I hope you've enjoyed this journey. It's been a long, hard road for me. I wanted to give it up so many times, but God would never let me. I knew it had to be done no matter how hard it got. I could never rest until this book was completed. I started to dream about what I might do after the book, but God said, "No." I thought about having a baby, or at least trying for one, or maybe adoption. Maybe I could go to seminary. "No." God made it very clear that I was to make no plans beyond this book. I don't really know why. Maybe it was because this book was so important that my focus was to be solely on the task at hand. Dreaming about the future was futile because none of us know what the future holds.

I wanted another baby so desperately, but the time kept going by. I had just turned 39 when I first started the book, and as I sit here right now writing its epilogue, I'm about to turn 44. It certainly wouldn't be unheard of for someone my age to at least adopt a baby, and I have dreamed about that very thing so many times. When we were in Ethiopia, I thought the people there were so lovely and delicate in their features, and I thought that I would love to have a beautiful Ethiopian daughter someday. But not long after that a younger woman in my church who had gone on the trip to India with me announced she was adopting a little girl from there. I was nowhere near completion of the book at that time, but I thought that I could share in her happiness somehow. I felt such a connection with the people of Ethiopia. We share the common bond of suffering. It was so interesting to be there in that impoverished land and join them in their worship service where even the young women wept aloud as they prayed. They were crying out for God's healing and blessing that had so long eluded them, and I cried and prayed with them. My mother's maiden name is Cryer. It seems to be in my nature, a part of who I really am, a Cryer, a person who cries, or maybe a person who calls out to tell others the news. Isn't that what a town crier really did?

When my friend finally brought her daughter home and to church, I ran over to find them after the service. I wanted to hold her so badly, but they wouldn't let me. She had just entered a new country, and they, as her new parents, had to protect her, even from me. I still haven't held that baby, and that is how it is supposed to be. Something died in me that day when I was denied the fulfillment of the desire to hold a baby, but it was supposed to. This also was from God. That baby was for them, not me, not even for a second. If I had what I wanted, I would already have a Chinese baby girl and an Ethiopian one and maybe a little boy from Guatemala. Who knows? My heart is so fickle. But God had a plan and a purpose in my baby's dying, and one of those plans was this book. I can't make any plans for myself. God has made that clear. He lays the paths of my life. He leads; I follow. So I don't know what the future holds now that this book is near completion. Like the hymn, "How Deep the Father's Love for Us" reminds me, "But this I know with all my heart, His wounds have paid my ransom." And that is enough for me.

It's interesting that Ethiopia has a holiday on January 19. Their Epiphany commemorates the baptism of Jesus in the Jordan. If they're correct, Bronner, you and Jesus were baptized on the same day. I doubt they are because it's cold in January even in Israel. I know. That's when we went. But it's still a fitting example of the unity of God among His people throughout the world. I found a kinship in Ethiopia, a longing for something more, something lasting, something beautiful, and I found a holiday there that blessed my soul knowing that there is nothing on earth that is random or haphazard. But God works and weaves us together in such a way that is so mysterious and wonderful that I cannot help but cry, "Holy." He is so beyond comprehension, so beyond my grasp, but I make it my lifelong goal to try, to grasp at even the hem of His garment, to study and ponder and search out everything He has for me.

My former babysitter, Lindsey, to whom I introduced you in chapter 1, is having a baby, her first. I rounded up every stitch of maternity clothing I own and boxed it up for her. She still says she's naming her baby Bronner if she has a boy. We'll see. I hope so. Lindsey told me she prayed that she will love her own baby as much as she loves Bronner. I know that seems crazy for anyone to love someone else's baby that much, but I believe she did and does. Lindsey is a rare and beautiful person, filled with love and grace, and I am honored to have her as part of my life and Bronner's. Those maternity clothes belong with her.

Although I still believe I am young enough to have more children, I am not convinced that Rick is. He turns 50 very soon, and by the time of publication, I'm sure he will already be 50. And although he is still so filled with life and joy and peace, the years have worn on him. He has raised Brandi and Blake. He is raising Brooks and Brody. He has buried Bronner. And I'm just not sure he could do it again. But just when I thought I could say good-bye to my baby dreams, I see Blake, who is 23, with a girlfriend that at this moment he seems to love, and those dreams come rushing back. Life is so sweet even in its fallenness.

Indeed He does make everything beautiful in its time.

ACKNOWLEDGMENTS

First and foremost, I have to acknowledge that this is not my story, nor is it really even Bronner's story. It's God's from first to last. I originally titled this book simply *Bronner* because I didn't want to give too much away in the title. Bronner—how could that be threatening in any way? He was a beautiful little boy, beloved of his mother and father, sister and brothers. I never intended this to be a book on grief or only for those who are grieving but have always hoped it would be more of a biblical explanation for pain and suffering. And all of us who belong to Jesus will suffer. I hope that fact has been established. None of us who claim Christ will get an easy ride. Following Him means going where He has gone, to the Cross, and the Cross was no fun.

Secondly, I want to thank Brody and Brandi and Brooks and Blake, in that order, because I think that is the order in which my time away from them while writing this book was felt the most. Brody began having panic attacks and separation anxiety, so much so that I knew I could only write when he was at school or away for a fun beach trip or lacrosse tournament, or during something else he wouldn't miss me too much for. But it was more than that. He seemed to fear losing someone else in his family.

For most kids, life seems to go on forever, and those they love are ever near, or at least alive. But Brody knew differently. Bronner was gone, and if he had been taken from him, then that meant that it wasn't out of the realm of possibility that someone else could be taken. The person I believe he most feared losing was me, maybe because I wasn't there as much anymore, especially during the early stages of writing when I was doing most of the work at the farm.

Brandi had panic attacks, too, when she first went off to college. There were probably other factors at play, but there's no doubt that Bronner was a part of it. And Brandi needs me. I didn't get to go with Rick and the boys when they went to see her when she was living in New York. I needed the weekend to write. When it came right down to it, I had to make some sacrifices. I hope I can make up the time with them all. I want to be so involved that they get sick of seeing my face!

The two oldest boys have learned to lean on their daddy, and that is just the way it should be. I'm glad.

Now to some real helpers in this story: Donna Gilmore, Donna Gilmore, Donna Gilmore. Donna Gilmore was Brooks's sixth-grade teacher. I remember checking his papers (yes, I said *papers*, in sixth grade) for grammar and punctuation and thinking that everything was correct. (I did double-major in English and communication, you know.) Mrs. Gilmore thought wrong! I found out that she was the comma queen. I thought that might come in handy. I told her I was writing a book and asked would she mind looking it over as the chapters came along. She was more than willing to help. I sent her what I had and each chapter as I finished it, and, of course, she found commas out of place and grammatical errors galore! I was thankful. I'm from a small town in Alabama, and didn't want a publisher thinking I was a country bumpkin right out of the gate! So she was one of the very first people to read this very personal story. At first, it was hard to let anyone see it. It was just so close to my heart, but I knew she wouldn't think I was crazy—or at least I hoped not anyway. I sent it through the mail, mainly, and she would send it back.

Brody got another teacher for sixth grade, so I didn't see Mrs. Gilmore much. But when I finally did go to her classroom the day Brody graduated from sixth grade, we had such a sweet embrace that we must have made a spectacle of ourselves in front of a classroom full of students and their parents. Not many people even knew I was writing a book at that point, and I don't think anyone outside of maybe a handful knew she was helping me edit it. So, thank you, Donna, from the bottom of my heart. I hope you know how much I love and trust you.

I also want to thank all the wonderful women in my neighborhood who helped carpool my boys to school and back so many times, and even one dad who drove Brody every day for a year. I especially want to thank Wendy Morris for this. I learned only after Bronner went to heaven that neighbors really do want to be neighborly and help you with your kids when you need them. I wish I had known this before.

Thank you to David Sanford, who patiently waited for this manuscript through the years. He assured me that he could get this published with no problem, even before he read one word of it. He understood that I didn't want the pressure of a deadline and needed to go this journey mostly alone. He believed in this book from the very beginning. David met with Rick and me and told us how he could feel God's hand upon it. He felt it was ordained by God. He seemed to say he knew that it was. I certainly did.

And, of course, I want to acknowledge Rick in this. His positive assurances, with each chapter completed, kept me on track. So many times I would wonder if I was making any sense at all, but he backed up every word. If anyone wonders if Rick sees things this way as well, wonder no more. He agrees with every word written here. In fact, much of it is his part in the story, what God said to and through him. We both love Bronner so much. We both love all of our children so much. It's a tearful thing to have children. They're so much joy and pain wrapped up together. Every tear they cry, we cry with them. It's like a little part of you, as all of you fellow parents well know, walking around exploring the world through different eyes. And Rick is such a good dad—the best, really. He's so much fun, and he puts everything in perspective, summing it all up in a nice, neat sound bite. He cuts to the chase and puts everyone at ease. Many of you have heard him on the radio or at a men's event or an outdoor expo. You know he can be a lot of fun.

What you may not know is how serious Rick can be and how deeply he loves the Lord. What I know about Rick is that he is truly pure in heart. He loves God with such fervor and without a hint of doubt or reservation. A man like that can be trusted. When he speaks, people listen. I listen. So when he says that this book is good, I know he really means it. So thank you, sweet, precious husband, for believing in me, encouraging me, and never letting me quit. I'm so glad I didn't. This book is as much yours as it is mine. I love you as much as any wife has ever loved her husband. And why not? You're terrific!

Last but not least, I want to thank Maegan Roper, Joyce Dinkins, and everyone at New Hope Publishers. When Joyce wanted to take our shoes off for a picture at my contract signing because of the weight of God's presence and His plan for this book, I knew I was in the right place. I thought, "Now, this is someone I can relate to!" I knew I was meeting a kindred spirit who understands how God's Spirit works inside a person to compel them toward a specific calling. The message of this book was ordained by God, and I am so thankful that this group of God-fearing, Spirit-filled people was the one who would ultimately see it through to publication. And what a joy it truly has been.

Forever grateful,

READER'S GUIDE

*A supplement for personal growth and life application to
be used as individual study or group discussion guide*

I open *Bronner: A Journey to Understand* with Psalm 40:1–3 because
these three verses encapsulate the theme of this book so well. I
cried out to the Lord, and He answered me. He crushed me to the
uttermost when, in His divine providence and will, He took my
son into heaven with Him. But God drew me up out of that pit of
destruction and made my faith so much stronger than it had been
before. I now walk this valley of the shadow of death without fear
and with a song of praise to my God in my heart. It is my great
hope that many will see what the Lord has done and put their trust
in Him.

Read Psalm 40:1–3. Can you remember a time when God lifted you up
from a difficult situation and brought joy back into your heart? If so, take a
moment to thank Him for it.

Consider the words of Romans 8:28. Do you truly believe that God can bring
good into any situation or circumstance you find yourself in?

According to Proverbs 3:5, we are to trust God with our whole hearts.
Ask yourself, in all sincerity, if you do. If yes, you are on your way to that

unshakable faith that God so desires of you. If not, what are some steps you can take to deepen your trust in the Lord?

Do you recall what Genesis records happened to the young man named Joseph? (Optional: read his full story in Genesis 37 and 39–50.) In brief, Joseph was cast into a pit by his brothers and sold into slavery. Later, Joseph endured prison after being falsely accused, but in the end, he became a great and trusted ruler, leader, and savior for his people. At this point, Joseph's brothers discovered his fate and were afraid. Record what Joseph said to his brothers in Genesis 45:5–8 and 50:20 to comfort them.

Do you believe it is possible that your difficult situation could help save lives from an eternal perspective?

Have you ever really thought about hell and what it must be like? Can you imagine your neighbor or friend there? I shiver to think of anyone there, but God's Word tells us that there will be many who find themselves in that place of "weeping and gnashing of teeth" (Matthew 8:12).

Read Matthew 7:13–14. Fill in the blanks: "Enter by the narrow gate. For the gate is _____ and the way is _____ that leads to destruction, and those who enter by it are _____ . For the gate is _____ and the way is _____ that leads to life, and those who find it are _____ .

The contrast between these two gates is stark. Have you entered the narrow gate, and if so, are you willing to go through some hard stuff here on earth in order to help others find that gate that leads to (eternal) life?

CHAPTER I

A Crown of Great Worth

If pride was the original sin (Ezekiel 28:13–17), doesn't it take some humility to become righteous? The prideful man trusts in himself; the humble person sees his shortcomings and hopes for deliverance from sin. It takes humility to admit, "I can't do it on my own" and to say, "I need a Savior." Humility is the first step to becoming a Christian, and it is a companion discipline to any future growth in that Christian.

Psalm 149:4; Proverbs 3:34; and Isaiah 66:2 all tout benefits of being humble. What do these verses say the Lord will do for those who are humble?

• *With these promises in mind, is it any wonder why God sometimes chooses to humble us?*

Read Daniel 4:28–37. What happened to the great king of Babylon, Nebuchadnezzar, when he looked out upon his kingdom and gloried in it?

• *To what did Nebuchadnezzar give credit for building his kingdom? (v. 30)*

• *After Nebuchadnezzar's humiliation, what was his attitude then, and whom was he praising? (vv. 34–37)*

• *In verse 37, what does Nebuchadnezzar say that God is able to do for those who walk in pride?*

Who is our ultimate example of humility? (See Philippians 2:5–10.)

Don't live your life for the wrong world. Be a humble human and wait on God. He promises to exalt the humble but not until the proper time (1 Peter 5:6–10). Just wait. There is a crown waiting on you in heaven (2 Timothy 4:7–8). Don't blow eternity on what is fading away (Isaiah 40:6–8; 2 Peter 3:10–13).

Read Hebrews 11:13–16. Did the faith heroes from Hebrews 11 see the earth as a homeland?

What land were they really seeking?

Do you believe heaven holds more treasure for the Christian than the earth? If so, are you living your life in a way that reflects that belief?

CHAPTER 2

Hearts Made Ready

Even though the Bible tells us to expect a fiery trial (1 Peter 4:12), we never really do. I believe the reason we don't expect calamity in our lives is that we were created for something greater than this fallen world. We were created for God, to live in the light of His presence. And, for the saint who has tasted of His goodness and grace, this present darkness will never be good enough. Our hearts soar to great heights of hope and peace and patience knowing God, the Father, loves us fully, compassionately, and unwaveringly.

It is my firmly held belief that the greatest strides in our faith walk come through our suffering, but I also firmly believe that unless we are rooted and grounded in faith beforehand, before the great storms of life hit, we are likely to fall and fall hard. Read Matthew 7:24–27 and summarize.

Study Psalm 1:1–3. The Hebrew word esher is translated here as "blessed." Esher also denotes happiness. What does this happy and blessed person take delight in?

What does the psalmist mean when he says the person he is describing is "like a tree planted by streams of water" yielding fruit and keeping its leaves green and healthy throughout life?

What do you suppose is the key to this person's fruitful life, and how much time do you spend in those same pursuits?

What promises from Proverbs 2:6–8 mean the most to you?

From those same verses, what is our part in gaining wisdom, and what responsibility do we have in our relationship with God?

Read 1 John 1:5; 4:8; and Psalm 38:9. What are the three characteristics of God we find in these verses?

How well do you reflect those qualities of God? Is there room for improvement, and if so, what can you do to begin growing in these godly traits?

Consider Job's suffering. He lost all his livestock, many of his servants, and all his sons and daughters in one day. Then he was struck with "loathsome sores from the sole of his foot to the crown of his head" (Job 2:7). In all of this, Job did not sin and famously said, "Naked I came from my mother's womb, and naked shall I return. The LORD gave, and the LORD has taken away; blessed be the name of the LORD" (1:21). He chides his wife asking, "Shall we receive good from God, and shall we not receive evil?" (2:10). Read Job 1:1. What kind of man was Job before his affliction?

Do you think he could have responded in the same way if he had not already had a faithful walk with God?

It is never too late to start walking in step with God. We all have great strides to make in pursuing godliness, integrity, wisdom, and virtue. Will you commit your life to these pursuits right now, today?

CHAPTER 3

The Coldest, Darkest Night

Jesus said, "In this world you will have trouble. But take heart! I have overcome the world" (John 16:33 NIV). The King James Version of that verse uses the phrase "be of good cheer" in the place of "take heart." Jesus wanted to encourage us in times of distress that He had overcome the world, and in doing so had conquered it, laid claim on it, and taken it back from Satan. The earth is the Lord's. He created it, and it belongs to Him. But when sin entered into the world, it became corrupted. What Jesus had overcome was that corruption. He had lived a sinless life and was about to take on death on the Cross and claim victory for all of us who would believe in Him. That is why Paul could write that we are more than conquerors in all of these things: tribulation, distress, persecution, famine, nakedness, danger, and sword (Romans 8:35–37). Jesus has not only conquered sin and death, He has overcome them, swallowed them up in victory banishing them forever.

Read Revelation 20:11–21:5. What is going to happen to death in the end? (20:14; 21:4)

Who will wipe away our tears? (21:4)

From 21:1–5, what are you looking forward to the most?

In times of grief or despair, we are sometimes tempted to wonder what we did wrong to deserve such punishment, but Romans 8:1 declares that for those who are in Christ Jesus, there is no condemnation. Write out Romans 8:1.

Read Hebrews 12:1–11. Discipline is not the same thing as punishment and definitely not condemnation. God's discipline is training in righteousness (v. 11). Jesus is not only the founder of our faith, He is its perfecter (v. 2). From verse 10, what does God want to share with us through discipline?

Study Romans 5:3–4 and James 1:2–3, and list the virtues gained through suffering named in these verses.

In 2 Corinthians 1:8–9, Paul says he was so afflicted that he felt he had been given "the sentence of death," but there was a reason for that. What was it, and do you believe the afflictions you face in life can have the same effect?

In 12:1–10, Paul says that he had been given visions of heaven so great that God gave him a thorn in his side so he wouldn't be overly elated by them. Paul asked that the thorn (not a literal thorn but possibly some form of sickness, some suggest an eye disease) be taken away. What was God's response to Paul (v. 9)?

Why does Paul, in verse 10, say that he is content with "weaknesses, insults, hardships, persecutions, and calamities"?

Read 4:7–12 and 16–18. Paul says in verses 7–12 that the reason he is taken to the brink of despair but never fully there (he is afflicted, perplexed, persecuted, and struck down but never crushed, forsaken, or destroyed) is simply that the gospel can go forth in power but also that Paul's life can more and more mirror the life of Jesus. The result of this is given in verses 16–17. He calls his suffering "a light momentary affliction" (v. 17) because he knew it was only temporary. What was he looking to that gave him the motivation to keep going (v. 18)?

Romans 8:16–17 is a provisional statement and a profound one. What does it say we must do in order to be glorified with Christ?

If the statement in Romans 8:16–17 is true, then we truly should count suffering as joy. It may not be pleasant at the moment, but we know that after this race is run, there will be room for nothing but joy. Can you wait for it with patience and in the meantime work diligently as "a good soldier of Christ Jesus" (2 Timothy 2:3), bearing all things for His name's sake and for the kingdom that is coming?

CHAPTER 4

A Father's Heart

"Satan, you lose! You are not going to win this!" Rick Burgess was ready to fight when he was brought into action. He was like a valiant knight on a glorious quest for his King. First, he wanted to make sure his lady was safe and taken care of, but then his attention turned to the battlefront. He began pointing people to God through the loss of his son from the very beginning, and he hasn't stopped. The Spirit of God within him began working immediately to use what Satan meant for harm for God's good purposes.

Carefully consider Ephesians 5:10–20. List some of the ways we can all be prepared to go into battle when the Lord calls us to the front lines.

Rick's response to this storm wasn't human, but spiritual. Study Romans 8:3–15. What do those who live according to God's Spirit set their minds on (v. 5)? Give examples.

Those who live to gratify the flesh are hostile to God and His law (v. 7) and therefore cannot please Him (v. 8). Those who belong to God through faith in Jesus Christ live their lives in order that they may please God. Ask yourself if your Father's heart is enough for you. Is pleasing God truly the aim of your life? If not, would you like it to be?

Read John 14. How many times in this beautiful chapter of the Bible does Jesus tell us the way we show our love for Him? List the verses where you find your answers, underline them in your Bible, and summarize them into one statement.

Look up the Great Commission given in Matthew 28:18–20. What is the three-part command given?

From 2 Corinthians 5:17–21, what ministry have we been given as ambassadors for Christ? Is this ministry for a select few, or is this for all who are in Christ?

In the midst of pain and suffering, God's Spirit says to press on. He gives strength, comfort, and love. A human response would be to give up, be angry, and despair. Read 1 Corinthians 15:56–58. How do these verses encourage you?

CHAPTER 5

But I Want You To Be Holy

After Bronner went heaven, I spent so much time alone in prayer. I knew God held the answers, and I was desperate to understand why this had to be. He answered me. I said to God, "But we were so happy; we were so happy, God." And He said, "But I want you to be holy." It was a clear directive to make the aim of my life something deeper than it had been before. I wanted to know everything I could about holiness. I found that the first time we see the word holy in the Bible is in Genesis 2:3, as God is talking about a day that would be different from all the other days.

Read Genesis 2:3. Based on this verse alone, what can we know about the word holy, and how can we apply that knowledge to our lives today? (Note: some Bible versions use the word sanctified for holy here.)

Leviticus is a book of the law, and reading it greatly deepens our concept of holiness. Again and again in this sacred book, God tells His people to "be holy, for I am holy" (Leviticus 11:44, 45; 20:7, 26). Many times, God follows this command with rules and laws concerning behavior and morality, giving us a picture of His standard of what is right and acceptable and what is not. Read Leviticus 20:7–8. How do these verses add to your understanding of what it means to be holy?

Lest we feel that being holy is an Old Testament command and not applicable to the modern Christian, please read 1 Peter 1:14–16, and give a summary of those verses in your own words.

Hebrews 12:14 is perhaps the most convicting and sobering verse on holiness in the Bible. What does it say the lack of holiness will prevent a person from ever doing?

When we accept Jesus as Savior and Lord, His holiness is imparted to us by the redemptive power of Christ's obedience and sacrifice on the Cross. There is nothing we can do to earn this justification (or standing) before our holy God. But once we repent, or turn away from our sin, we are never to turn back and walk in those old ways again (Romans 6). We are ever after to strive for holiness (Hebrews 12:14), which according James is the living proof of our salvation (James 2:14–26). Keeping in mind that sanctification is just a way of saying "to be made holy," what is God's will for us and what has our salvation called us to according to 1 Thessalonians 4:3–7?

There's no splitting hairs when it comes to 1 John 3:7–10. The phrase used here is "makes a practice of sinning," as opposed to a stumble or a sin quickly confessed and repented of. Christians need the abiding presence of the Holy Spirit in their lives to convict them of sin and draw them back to God's holiness throughout their lives (Romans 8:3–14). Read 1 John 3:7–10. This passage of Scripture makes it clear who belongs to God and who does not. According to verse 10, how will it be evident who are the children of God?

Scripture uses the word happy to describe times of well-being and pleasant circumstances for God's people. Our lives will be filled with both happiness and sorrow, but the greater expression of delight in God, whatever our state of affairs, is joy, which comes to us not through events or conditions but through the Holy Spirit (Galatians 5:22–23). What other manifestations of the Spirit are found in these verses?

Whereas happiness can depend on a given situation or occurrence and therefore can come and go, joy seems to be commanded of the Christian no matter what is going on in our lives. Look up Philippians 4:4 in your Bible. What, or who, are we to rejoice in?

Keeping Philippians 4:4 in mind, how can holiness lead to happiness in your life?

CHAPTER 6
Children of a Brokenhearted Parent

"I wish it had been me, so you would still have Bronner to snuggle." It was the sweetest, kindest, most Christlike thing anyone has ever said to me before or since. Brooks loved me that much. His little nine-year-old heart was so pure and true and devoted to me, his mother, that he would have been willing even to die for me if that's what it would take to make me happy again. And I realized that

that kind of self-sacrificing love and loyalty is what God desires from me, from you, from all of His children.

Luke 15 contains three parables that emphasize the importance of one human soul and the great lengths God will go to in order to save it. Read Luke 15 and answer the following questions on the parables of the lost sheep, the lost coin, and the prodigal son:

- *In verses 3–7, the shepherd leaves the 99 sheep that are safe in order to go after the one that is not. Why would he do that?*
- *Do you think he should have stayed with the majority in order that they may remain safe, or do you think he does the right thing?*
- *What does the shepherd do when he finds the lost sheep?*
- *Does this short parable make you feel differently about the lost person you may know?*
- *How do you think God feels about that person?*
- *In the parable of the lost coin (vv. 8–10), how much trouble does the woman go through to find the missing coin?*
- *When does she stop seeking the lost coin?*
- *What does she do when she finds the coin, and would you have the same reaction over a person you helped lead to Christ even if that meant great personal sacrifice to you?*
- *In the parable of the prodigal son, we find two sinful sons, one overtly sinful and the other more inwardly sinful. Which one reflects your life most accurately?*
- *In verses 17–19, the younger son believed his actions had disqualified him as a son to his father, but in his humble condition, he knew his father was his only hope. Look back on your life. Have you ever felt this way before?*

Verse 20 is my favorite in this chapter. It tells me that even while I am still a long way off from God, He sees me, and if I take just the slightest step toward Him, He'll run to me and take me up into His arms and kiss me with His presence. I don't ever want to forget that. Do you?

While we love to think of God's compassion when it comes to our own lives, we don't always feel that way about others. Like the older son in the parable, we want justice to be done to that awful person who has wronged us, slighted us, or hurt us in any way, but can we today put God's feelings before our own and do whatever it takes to show a lost sinner his way home to God? And then can we be forgiving and celebrate with God that He has joy because His son or daughter, our brother or sister, has crossed over from death unto life?

When I beseeched God, desperately crying out to Him to tell me why, why the children, I heard Him say to me, "They're all mine. You're going to get this glorious reunion with your son, but I won't get that with all of mine." And maybe for the first time ever, I had compassion for God. It was then that I submitted to His will that my "light momentary affliction" (2 Corinthians 4:17) be used to bring some of God's lost sheep home to Him forever, thus bringing joy to the Lord and to the angels in heaven.

I pray that whatever hard thing is going on in your life can be used in this way as well. I will also pray that we will always love God enough to want to see Him celebrate and be joyful and that we will allow His joy to bring us strength in whatever circumstances of life we find ourselves in.

CHAPTER 7

Faith—Tested, Genuine, and Precious

Abraham was a man of great faith. He believed in God's promises, obeyed His Word, and took time to fellowship with God, yet God chose to test Abraham. I believe God took away my son for the same reason he asked Abraham to sacrifice his—to enlarge my faith and deepen my trust in Him; to make me holy, humble, and heaven-focused; and for the testimony of faith that would bring glory to God and many to salvation.

Hebrews 11:1 gives us a great definition of faith. Write out Hebrews 11:1.

What did God count as righteousness to Abram (Abraham) in Genesis 15:6?

Read Romans 3:22–25 and John 3:16, and answer the following questions.
* *Who can come to faith in Jesus Christ?*
* *What is the great reward of faith?*

From 1 Peter 1:6–7, what does the apostle tell us we are to rejoice in?

For what reason? (v. 7)

What is the word used in 1 Peter 1:7 to describe faith that has been tested and proven itself genuine?

Who do you think genuine faith is precious to?

Study 1 Peter 4:1–2 and 12–13, and answer the following questions.
* *What are we not supposed to be surprised at? (v. 12)*
* *What kind of life ought the person who has suffered to live? (v. 1)*
* *Instead of living for self or "human passions," the person whose faith has been refined by fire (trial) should now live for what? (v. 2)*

Who does 1 Peter 2:21 tell us has been left as an example to follow in suffering?

List the seven qualities 2 Peter 1:5–7 records as ones we are to "make every effort" to add to our faith.

According to 2 Peter 1:8–11, what are three benefits of increasing in the seven attributes you listed above?

Sincerely search yourself to see where you are in your faith walk with God. Are you growing? Are you making every effort to add to your faith the seven qualities listed in 2 Peter 1:5–7? Put a star beside the attributes from the list in which you feel you're doing a good job or are making strides in, and circle the ones you want to begin working on.

Or maybe you've never really taken that first step of faith. Why not take it now by praying something like this?

> God, I need You. I'm a mess without You. I've been try-ing to live life on my own, and I realize now that I can't and that I don't have to. I know You're there listening. I believe in You, and I trust in Your plans for me. I believe Jesus took the penalty of death upon Himself so I can live forever. I will die an earthly death one day, but I don't fear it because I know I will come to You in heaven. I also know that life here on earth may at times be difficult, even as a believer in Christ, so I ask that You be with me to guide and comfort me through Your Holy Spirit all of my days. In Jesus' name, amen.

If you have just prayed to receive Christ as Lord and Savior, please know that this is just the beginning of a life filled with joy and peace and relationship. I strongly suggest you join a local church to learn more about this new life you are embarking on. God bless you in your journey!

CHAPTERS 8 AND 9
Water and the Spirit and *Sevens*
A Combined Lesson on God's Comfort
God's comfort is sweet and, oh, so personal. For me, that included dragonflies, mourning doves, and sevens, but I have heard of bunnies and bumblebees, little yellow butterflies, and a van full of purple flowers for others. God can use anything to comfort us, for "the earth is the LORD's" and all things serve Him (Psalm 24:1). Yes, God puts us in the refining fires of the furnace of affliction, but He promises to be there with us through it all. He will never leave us nor forsake us. Indeed, no one teaches like the Lord, but He is faithful and worthy of our trust. And we can count on Him to calm the storms of our lives.

Read Matthew 8:23–27. What is the most notable part of this passage to you?

Scripture reads, "and there was a great calm" (v. 26). Something extraordinary happens when Jesus shows up. There was nothing ordinary about this miracle. Is it any less extraordinary that He can soothe and still our hearts in Him in the same way?

First Peter 5:6–10 contains exhortation, encouragement, comfort, and promise. In these verses, what means the most to you right now?

Read Daniel 3. Who do you think was in the fiery furnace with Shadrach, Meshach, and Abednego? What evidence from Scripture—and also from your own personal experience—makes you believe this?

- The three young men were bold in their conviction to worship God alone and were willing to face death rather than compromise what they knew to be right. What effect did their unwavering faith have on the king?
- Record what Nebuchadnezzar said of God after all was said and done.
- Would you like to think that others can see how God has rescued you from the pit of destruction and despair and give glory to God in heaven?

Read 2 Corinthians 1:3–5. God "comforts us in all our affliction." In turn, we are able to comfort others with the same comfort we have been given from the Lord.

- Who do these verses say we can comfort? Are we limited to those who have suffered in the same way we have?
- Does it help you to know that your pain is not in vain and that it can be used to help someone else in some way?

We can glean much comfort from the Book of Psalms. The familiar Shepherd's Psalm soothed my soul like no other from the very beginning, as it still does today. What from Psalm 23 is the greatest help to you?

Study Psalm 139:1–18. How does it make you feel to know that God is so intimately acquainted with all your ways, that His eyes have never once left you, and that all of your days were formed for you before there was one of them?

Psalm 34:18–19, 22; 36:7; and 46:1 all convey the idea of God as our refuge and help in times of trouble. I remember curling up with God and allowing Him to comfort me with His presence and promises time after time. Read these verses from Psalms, and summarize how each of these has proven true in your life.

Read Isaiah 61:1–3. Do you believe God can bind up your broken heart and give you gladness instead of mourning, beauty from ashes, and praise instead of a faint spirit?

When Bronner went to heaven, I was afraid. I didn't know the world could be that bad, but God has brought peace through understanding, hope through His promises, deep comfort, and solid confirmation. Trust Him to do the same for you.

CHAPTER 10

The Living Will Lay It to Heart

Ecclesiastes has always been one of my favorite books of the Bible. It is a book filled with wisdom written by the wisest of kings (1 Kings 4:29, 34). In Ecclesiastes, King Solomon, who calls himself "the Preacher," seeks to find the meaning and purpose behind life "under the sun" (Ecclesiastes 1:2–3). After all of his searching, he concludes that life is utterly meaningless apart from God and sums up the whole matter with one dictate: "Fear God and keep his commandments, for this is the whole duty of man" (12:13). But Solomon has much to impart between the first and last chapters of this compact book of the Bible.

What event is Solomon referring to in Ecclesiastes 2:14 that happens to both the wise and the foolish?

Read Genesis 2:15–17 and 3:1–6. What caused death to enter into the world?

After completing this book and the accompanying reader's guide, do you feel you better understand why God allowed Satan to test humanity in the first place?

Do you believe that the testing of your faith and trust in God will make you a more thankful and loyal servant and friend of God in the ages to come?

How can death point to the power of God and stir in us awe for His authority and majesty?

If death has separated you from someone you love, what has God taught you about Himself through your pain, and has your faith grown or diminished because of this loss?

Read Ecclesiastes 7:1–14, and answer the following questions.
- *How can the day of death be better than the day of birth?*
- *In what way is sorrow better than laughter?*
- *How can we reconcile God's goodness with His ultimate sovereignty over life and death? In other words, if we believe that God is both good and sovereign, can we conclude that God's plans for us in both life and in death are good?*

Read 2 Peter 3:10–14; Ephesians 2:10; and James 2:14–26. From these passages, what are we to be doing in the meantime, between our salvation and the time that God calls us to Himself in heaven?

Are you ready to put your working boots on and make your life count for the Lord in this time and in this age?

EPILOGUE

I want to leave you with the main points of this book in a compact list that you can go back to for encouragement when you need to. Each point gives a reason why God allows pain and suffering. You may be going through a trial or major test of faith yourself, or you may know someone who is and want to understand why. We want to ease the suffering of others, but God holds them in the fire until they have learned His ways. Still some of you may be experiencing tremendous blessing, and this, too, is from the Lord. Enjoy it and be glad, but learn these lessons from those of us who have suffered so that you may not have to endure our same types of suffering, and if I can do that for you, it will all be worth it.

God tests us to refine us:
- *to melt away the dross of worldliness, pride, and self-reliance.*
- *to fit us for heaven and clothe us in righteousness, peace, and joy in the Holy Spirit.*
- *to create in us a fearlessness and boldness for God and the things of God.*
- *to bring us into a closer relationship and understanding of Himself.*
- *to make us hunger for more than this world can offer.*
- *to make us see God for who He really is—to be in awe of His holiness, majesty, and grace—and to see ourselves in perspective to His power and perfection—in other words, to humble us.*
- *to create in us a testimony of faith that brings glory to God and attracts others to His kingdom.*
- *to make us holy like Him—proven, faithful servants of God who are ready for a forever with Him.*

And that's what I'm in this for, forever. Aren't you?

The fires of trial, sorrow, and pain in our lives burn away apathy and are meant to create in us a new fire, a fire that burns deep down in our souls for God. Let's be sold-out, on-fire Christians that light a flame in our generation for God that will never go out.

God be with as you go.

With love and prayers,

SCRIPTURE INDEX

OTHER TITLES TO INSPIRE YOUR FAITH JOURNEY...

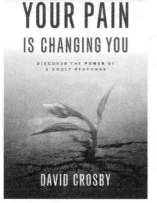

Your Pain Is Changing You

Discover the Power of a Godly Response

ISBN: 978-1-59669-413-2
$14.99

Upside-Down Joy

*An Inverted Look at Sin,
Sickness, Struggle, and Death*

ISBN: 978-1-59669-440-8
$14.99

For more information about these books and to read sample chapters
and more, visit NewHopePublishers.com

WorldCrafts℠ develops sustainable, fair-trade businesses among impoverished people around the world. Each WorldCrafts product represents lives changed by the opportunity to earn an income with dignity and to hear the offer of everlasting life.

Visit WorldCrafts.org to learn more about WorldCrafts artisans, hosting WorldCrafts parties and to shop!

WORLDCRAFTS℠
Committed. Holistic. Fair Trade.
WorldCrafts.org 1-800-968-7301

WorldCrafts is a division of WMU®.